Table of Contents

Introduction, My Personal Journey .... i-v
Year Round 1-52
Spring 53-82
Summer 83-120
Fall 121-156
Winter 157-192
Index 193

My Personal Journey

I am lazy, a horrible gardener, hate to cook or plan meals, and my family is very picky about food. Not a cookbook author candidate. But, I love my family, the Lord, and nutrition, and I committed to the Lord that I was going to find a way to prepare quick, easy, nutritious and tasty meals. Through faith and prayer, He led me to do this cookbook for myself and family.

In July 2000, I completed this book, spending 8 months of my precious free time – my girls were 3 and 1 ½ then – reading, researching, compiling, experimenting, and typing. I printed a hard copy to send to publishers, and then it was accidentally erased off my computer, irretrievable. I grieved and was angry, but I am now grateful. I've added and taken things out, and this book is better for it. I retyped from my one hard copy, backed up everything, raised money to self-publish, and five years and two babies later… voila!

Growing up, the Spirit told me there were ways to prevent ailments that my loved ones were experiencing. My nutrition fixation didn't begin until my first pregnancy, though. I knew nothing about the birth year, which was a blessing; there were no myths to deprogram myself from. I obsessed, ensuring that my baby would be the smartest, healthiest baby ever and I would be a good mother. It was soon revealed that those things were based on nutrition, lifestyle and avoiding unnecessary birth interventions. After I delivered, my passion for the birth year and parenting continued, and I became a doula and childbirth

A World of Wisdom

Seasonal Grain-based
Low Animal Product
Whole Foods Recipes

by Amy Cox Jones

Salt of the Earth Press - Springbrook, Wisconsin

ISBN: 978-0-9816949-1-7

Edited by Caroline Dykstra
Printed in the USA
2007 Printing

Published by
Salt of the Earth Press
Springbrook, Wisconsin, USA

educator, practicing as the Lord allowed.

In everything I learn, teach, and do for growing families, one theme is constantly repeated. Without your health and proper nutrition, do not plan for an easy or healthy life conception, pregnancy, birth, breast feeding experience, postpartum, and child. There is much out there to complement the W.O.W., and two books I love are "Nutrition and Physical Degeneration" by Weston Price and "Lasagna Gardening" by Patricia Lanza.

The W.O.W. is "Given for a principle with promise, adapted to the capacity of the weak and the weakest of all saints…" (D&C 89:3). I testify that this verse means the W.O.W. applies to everyone, poor/rich, stupid/smart, lazy/motivated, healthy/sickly… if you call yourself LDS, you can't get out of this one. Embrace these liberating principles! Beware, though, Satan will try to thwart your efforts. Both the adversary and the Lord know that good health is the gateway to happiness and success. Foremost, make this a spiritual, faith-filled journey. You will see blessings untold and the uncovered hidden treasures will amaze you. Thank you to my friends that helped and lent an ear, and my beloved husband and children for their patience and inspiration.

The Word of Wisdom

Latter Day Saints have been admonished, through scripture and leaders, to follow the Word of Wisdom, D&C 89. Through the health awareness movement, more non-members than members live accordingly, unknowingly obeying God-given commandments. Very few members follow the nutritional aspects of the Word of Wisdom, not for lack of willingness, but more for a lack of know how.

Doctrine and Covenants 89

4. In consequence of evils and designs, which do and will exist in the hearts of conspiring men in the last days, I have warned you, and forewarned you, by giving unto you this word of wisdom…
10. …all wholesome herbs God hath ordained for the constitution, nature, and use of man.
11. Every herb in the season thereof, and every fruit in the season thereof, all these to be used with prudence and thanksgiving.

12. Yea, flesh also of the beasts and fowls of the air, I, the Lord, have ordained for the use of man with thanksgiving, nevertheless they are to be used sparingly;

13. ...they should not be used, only in times of winter, or of cold, or famine.

14. All grain is... to be the staff of life...

18. And all saints who remember to keep and do these sayings, walking in obedience to the commandments, shall receive health to their naval and marrow to their bones;

19. And shall find wisdom and great treasures of knowledge, even hidden treasures.

20. And shall run and not be weary, and shall walk and not faint.

21. And I, the Lord, ...promise, that the destroying angel shall pass by them... and not slay them.

As outlined in these verses, we have been told to eat: Produce in its season; meat and animal products sparingly, and only in times of winter, cold and/or famine; grain as the bulk of our dietary.

Additionally, leaders have advised to eat foods in original states, avoiding processing, refinement, etc. Therefore, we are also to eat whole foods.

Having transitioned from the "standard American diet" (S.A.D.) to a W.O.W. based one, I understand how to be successful. It is futile to just know the truths of the Word of Wisdom, you need tools to live accordingly. My prayer is this cookbook will be one of those tools.

♦ Take your time.

A slow change is a permanent change. Don't overwhelm your body or family by quickly changing your eating. Gradually incorporating these principles will make for a joyous, easy journey.

♦ Don't be a Food Nazi

Allow an occasional treat at a birthday party, etc. Live The Spirit of the Word of Wisdom. Negative motivators like guilt, fear, control, etc., will drive the Spirit away and defeat your purpose, and may lead to destructive eating behaviors and mindsets. Your example and attitude is of utmost importance.

- Be patient in seeing results and blessings. Some are immediate, others can take months or years.
- Pray for strength, faith, and endurance.

  Your body and palate has grown accustomed to processed and sugared foods, therefore you're going to crave them. You may also detoxify, evidenced with flu-like symptoms, especially if you were a heavy junk food eater. Trust that you will get your required nutrients without an excess of milk and meat. There are huge mental adjustments. Have faith that the Lord knows what He's doing.

- Shop farmer's markets and/or start a garden.

  The easiest way to know local seasonal produce is to shop farmer's markets, or start a garden or co-op, fulfilling another prophetic commandment. Produce nutrients are maximized by eliminating extreme temperature changes in shipment, eating organically, and consuming what is native in that particular season.

> The foods used by... modern people yield a short-age... of many necessary food factors, especially of vitamins and minerals... because so much... is preserved, salted, sugared, purified, polished, pickled, canned, extracted, concentrated, heated, dried, frozen, thawed, stored, packaged, processed, and refined! ...The Word of Wisdom warns against the "evils and design which do and will exist in the hearts of conspiring men in the last days."
>
> *Apostle J.A.Widtsoe, 1950*

Since 1950 animal hormones and antibiotics and forced cycles, plant and feed pesticides, herbicides and fungicides, are included in that list, in my opinion. Please be prayerful about growing/buying organic, non-genetically engineered (GMO's) food and seed when possible. If you exercise faith and creative budgeting, you will incur no added expense.

Through work and the Lord's guidance, an organic garden can be achieved and maintained in most areas. Invest in a good organic gardening book and trust the Lord. Respect nature, don't alter and abuse it, and food will grow the way the Lord intended, in their seasons, with the right balance of nutrients, without harmful and synthetic chemicals.

Many recent studies show that organic foods are 20-50% more nutritious than their conventionally grown counterparts. For example, one organic apple nutritionally equals one and a half conventionally grown apples. So, eat organically for the best value for your dollar.

♦ If it isn't a direct result of the earth's goodness, beware.

When considering prepared foods, if it can't be traced to its "roots" in three to four steps, think twice. For example, fruit in a fruit smoothie is not in its original state, so go through its history. The food came from the earth, and went to:

1. The blender. Nothing added or taken away to change its nutritional integrity. Therefore, it's only one step away "from the earth."

♦ Wisely the Lord has provided foods in differing regions at differing times.

The people of that region need the nutrients in their native foods, ripe in their seasons, to thrive. This cookbook is a guideline, not a script, to what is ripe in any season and area, therefore you may need to make adjustments accordingly.

♦ Milk and eggs have seasons!

Through research I found the main seasons for dairy are spring and fall. Milk and eggs are still naturally obtained in very hot or cold weather, but not abundantly or with good quality, unless you artificially intervene in natural cycles.

I promise that by living the Word of Wisdom nutritionally, you will find "wisdom and great treasures of knowledge, even hidden treasures," have increased "health to their naval and marrow to their bones," and "run and not be weary," and shall "walk and not faint" as the Lord has promised. You will bless future generations by increasing their knowledge and health, whether you begin prenatally or later in life. I am so grateful for these blessings and the Lord's goodness in revealing this scripture, for I have experienced these blessings, and wish for all to receive these blessings.

Amy Cox Jones, 2005
WOWcookbook.com

Kale, Swiss Chard, Lettuce, Mushroom, Beet, Collard Greens, Apple, Orange,

Year Round

Year Round
Year Round Grains, Rice, and Beans

Amaranth

Ancient Aztec Grain
- ◆ I cup dry amaranth
- ◆ 3 cups water

Boil water. Add amaranth, simmer covered on low heat 25 minutes.

Barley, Pearled

- ◆ I cup pearled barley
- ◆ 3 cups water

Boil water. Add barley, simmer covered on low heat 35-45 minutes.

Barley, Whole

- ◆ I cup barley
- ◆ 3 cups water

Boil water. Add barley, simmer covered on low heat 90 minutes. Expands to four times its size. Reduce cooking time to 60 minutes if barley was soaked overnight. Sproutable.

Buckwheat, Whole

Not an actual wheat, but a rhubarb relative.
- ◆ I cup whole buckwheat
- ◆ 3 cups water

Boil water. Add buckwheat, simmer covered on low heat 15-20 minutes. Sproutable.

Bulgar, Wheat

Also known as Parboiled Cracked Wheat.
- ◆ 1 cup bulgar
- ◆ 2 cups water

Boil water. Add bulgar, simmer covered on low heat 20 minutes.

Kamut

Egyptian Wheat.
- ◆ 1 cup kamut
- ◆ 3 cups water

Boil water. Add kamut, simmer covered on low heat 2 hours.
Sproutable.

Millet

One amino acid short of being a perfect food.
- ◆ 1 cup millet
- ◆ 3 cups water

Boil water. Add millet, simmer covered on low heat 35 minutes.

Oat Groats

This is what oatmeal is before being steamed and rolled.
- ◆ 1 cup oat groats
- ◆ 3 cups water

Boil water. Add oat groats, simmer covered on low heat 2 hours.
Reduce time to 80 minutes if groats were soaked overnight.
Sproutable.

Oats, Quick

Oat groats that have been cut, steamed and rolled.
- 1 cup quick oats
- 2 1/2 cups water

Boil water. Add oats, simmer covered on low heat 5-8 minutes. Some nutrition is lost through processing as compared to oat groats or steel cut oats.

Oats, Steel Cut

Inner portion of oat groats, cut into 2-3 pieces.
- 1 cup steel cut oats
- 3 cups water

Boil water. Simmer covered on low heat 30 minutes. Not as nutritious as oat groats.

Oats, Rolled

Steamed and rolled flat oat groats.
- 1 cup rolled oats
- 3 cups water

Boil water. Add oats, simmer covered on low heat 20 minutes.

"We need a generation of young people who, as Daniel, eat in a more healthy manner – and whose countenances show it."

President Ezra Taft Benson

Quinoa

Peruvian, pronounced keen wah, Incan mother grain.
- ♦ I cup black or white quinoa
- ♦ I 1/2 cup water

Put the quinoa into a fine strainer, and run water through it until the water is clear and no longer sudsy to remove bitter saphonins. If you don't have a fine strainer, rinse the quinoa in a bowl filled with water, and then pour it through a clean dishtowel. Prepackaged quinoa has usually been polished and pre-rinsed, but relying on preprocessing is risky.

Boil water. Add wet quinoa, simmer uncovered 12 minutes for white quinoa, 15 minutes for black. Quinoa is fully cooked when the germ has separated from the grain. It looks like a small white "C" shape surrounding each grain. If any excess liquid remains, pour it off and raise the head to quickly boil off the rest.

Rye Berries

- ♦ I cup rye berries
- ♦ 4 cups water

Boil water. Add rye, simmer uncovered on low heat for 90 minutes. Sproutable.

Spelt

Also known as Farro or Dinkel. Mesopotamian grain.
- ♦ I cup spelt
- ♦ 3 cups water

Boil water. Add spelt, simmer covered on low heat for 90 minutes. Sproutable. Spelt's husk protects it from pollutants and insects and usually allows growers to avoid using pesticides.

Teff Berries

Ethiopian grain. Smallest grain in the world.
- ◆ I cup teff
- ◆ 4 cups water

Boil water. Add teff, simmer covered on low heat for 15 minutes. Sproutable.

Wheat, Cracked

Whole wheat berries, cut in 2-3 pieces.
- ◆ I cup cracked wheat
- ◆ 2 1/2 cups water

Boil waiter. Add cracked wheat, simmer covered on low heat for 25 minutes.

Wheat Berries

Red Winter Wheat.
- ◆ I cup wheat
- ◆ 3 cups water

Boil water. Add wheat, simmer covered on low heat 2 hours. Reduce time to 50-60 minutes if soaked overnight. Sproutable.

Wheat – Thermos Method

- ◆ I cup wheat berries
- ◆ 2 cups boiling water

Combine wheat and boiling water in quart size thermos. Screw top on tightly and leave overnight. Thermos method is applicable to most grains and beans with adjustment to water and grain/bean ratios.

Wheat – Crockpot Method

◆ I cup wheat berries
◆ 2 cups water

Combine water and wheat. Cook 6 to 8 hours on low.

No Cooking/Raw Method for Grains, Rice and Beans

This method retains the most nutrients.

◆ Grains, rice or beans
◆ water

Cover desired amount of grain with water and let soak a day or two until softened. It will be crunchy, akin to nuts.

Arborio Rice

Italian short grain creamy rice.

◆ I cup arborio rice
◆ 2 1/2 cups water

Boil water. Add rice, simmer covered on low heat 25 minutes.

Basmati Brown Rice

◆ I cup brown basmati rice
◆ 2 1/2 cups water

Boil water. Add rice, simmer covered on low heat 45 minutes.
More nutritious than white basmati.

Basmati White Rice

Brown basmati, stripped of digestive endosperm.

◆ I cup white basmati rice
◆ I 3/4 cup water

Boil water. Add rice, simmer covered on low heat 15 minutes.

Brown Short Grain Rice

Jones' family rice preference.
- ◆ 1 cup short grain brown rice
- ◆ 2 cups water

Boil water. Add rice, simmer covered on low heat 30-35 minutes.

Brown Long and Medium Grain Rice

- ◆ 1 cup long or medium grain brown rice
- ◆ 2 cups water

Boil water. Add rice, simmer covered on low heat 45 minutes.

Jasmine Brown Rice

Long grain rice from Thailand.
- ◆ 1 cup brown jasmine rice
- ◆ 2 1/2 cups water

Boil water. Add rice, simmer covered on low heat 45 minutes.

Jasmine White Rice

Brown jasmine, stripped of digestive endosperm.
- ◆ 1 cup jasmine white rice
- ◆ 1 3/4 cup water

Boil water. Add rice, simmer covered on low heat 15 minutes.

Sushi Rice

Be sure to get talc free packaging.
- ◆ 1 cup sushi rice
- ◆ 2 cups water

Rinse rice until water runs clear, soak for 40 minutes. Boil water. Add rice, simmer covered on low heat 45 minutes. Let stand 10 minutes.

Sweet Rice

Brown rice version of sushi rice.
- ◆ I cup sweet rice
- ◆ I 1/2 cup water

Boil water. Add rice, simmer covered on low heat 45 minutes.

Wehani Rice

Also known as red rice. Nutritious, Indian basmati-type rice.
- ◆ I cup wehani rice
- ◆ 2 cups water

Boil water. Add rice, simmer covered on low heat 45 minutes.

Wild Rice

Actually a grass seed grain.
- ◆ I cup wild rice
- ◆ 4 cups water

Boil water. Add rice, simmer covered on low heat I hour.

Adzuki Beans

Japanese Bean.
- ◆ I cup adzuki beans
- ◆ 3 cups water

Do not soak. Boil water. Add beans, simmer covered on low heat 90 minutes. Sproutable.

Anasazi Beans

Southwestern U.S. Bean.
- ♦ I cup anasazi beans
- ♦ 4 cups water

Soak overnight. Boil water. Add beans, simmer covered on low heat 90 minutes. Sproutable.

Black Eyed Peas

- ♦ I cup black eyed peas
- ♦ 4 cups water

Soak overnight. Boil water. Add peas (beans), simmer covered on low heat I hour and I5 minutes. Sproutable.

Black Beans

- ♦ I cup black beans
- ♦ 3 cups water

Soak overnight. Boil water. Add beans, simmer covered on low heat 90 minutes. Sproutable.

Cranberry Beans

Also known as Borlotti beans.
- ♦ I cup cranberry beans
- ♦ 3 cups water

Soak overnight. Boil water. Add beans, simmer covered on low heat I hour I5 minutes. Sproutable.

Canelli Beans

Also known as white kidney bean.
- ◆ 1 cup canelli beans
- ◆ 3 cups water

Soak overnight. Boil water. Add beans, simmer uncovered on low heat 90 minutes.

Fava Beans

- ◆ 1 cup fava beans
- ◆ 4 cups water

Soak overnight. Peel skins. Boil water. Add beans, simmer covered on low heat 3 hours.

Garbanzo Beans

Also known as chickpeas or ceci.
- ◆ 1 cup garbanzo beans
- ◆ 4 cups water

Soak overnight. Boil water. Add beans, simmer covered on low heat 3 hours.

Great Nothern Beans

- ◆ 1 cup great northern beans
- ◆ 3 cups water

Soak overnight. Boil water. Add beans, simmer covered on low heat 2 hours.

Kidney Beans

- ◆ 1 cup kidney beans
- ◆ 4 cups water

Soak overnight. Boil water. Add beans, simmer covered on low heat 90 minutes.

Lentils

- ◆ 1 cup lentils, any variety
- ◆ 2 cups water

Do not soak. Boil water. Add beans, simmer covered on low heat 20-45 minutes, depending on variety.

Lima Bean

- ◆ 1 cup lima beans
- ◆ 2 cups water

Soak overnight. Boil water. Add beans, simmer covered on low heat 60-90 minutes, depending on if it's a baby or large lima bean.

Mung Bean

- ◆ 1 cup mung beans
- ◆ 4 cups water

Do not soak. Boil water. Add beans, simmer covered on low heat 1 hour 15 minutes.

Navy Beans

- ◆ 1 cup navy beans
- ◆ 4 cups water

Soak overnight. Boil water. Add beans, simmer covered on low heat 2 1/2 hours.

Peas, Whole

- ◆ I cup peas
- ◆ 3 cups water

Soak overnight. Boil water. Add peas, simmer covered on low heat 90 minutes.

Peas, Split

- ◆ I cup split peas
- ◆ 2 cups water

Do not soak. Boil water. Add peas, simmer covered on low heat 45 minutes.

Pinto Beans

- ◆ I cup pinto beans
- ◆ 4 cups water

Soak overnight. Boil water. Add beans, simmer covered on low heat 2 hours.

Red Beans

- ◆ I cup red beans
- ◆ 4 cups water

Soak overnight. Boil water. Add beans, simmer covered on low heat 2 hours.

Soy Beans – Beige or Black

- ◆ I cup soybeans
- ◆ 3 cups water

Soak overnight in refrigerator. Boil water. Add beans, simmer covered on low heat 3-4 hours. Must be cooked thoroughly.

Year Round Basics

Wheat Pasta – Eggless

- ◆ 3 cups wheat flour
- ◆ 1/2 teaspoon salt
- ◆ 1 cup plain yogurt

Combine 2 cups flour and salt in large bowl. Add yogurt and mix well. Add remaining flour and knead. Let rest 15 minutes. Roll out thinly on floured surface and let dry 1/2 hour. Dust with flour and roll up. Slice desired thickness and separate or use pasta maker. Cook in boiling water 4-5 minutes.

Wheat Pasta

- ◆ 3 eggs
- ◆ 1/4 cup water
- ◆ 1 teaspoon salt
- ◆ 2 1/2 cups wheat flour

Combine eggs, water and salt with fork. Add enough flour to make a medium to firm dough. Cover and rest 20 minutes. Roll out on floured surface and let dry 1/2 hour. Dust with flour and roll up. Slice desired thickness or use pasta maker. Boil water and cook 4-5 minutes, or dry the pasta and store it in an airtight container.

Flavored Noodles
- ◆ 1/4 cup any vegetable juice i.e. spinach, carrot, etc.

Substitute vegetable juice for water in above recipe. May also substitute seasonings for salt. Proceed as directed.

Multi Grain Pasta

- 1 cup wheat flour
- 1/4 cup millet or soy flour
- 1/4 cup buckwheat flour
- 2-3 eggs
- 3 tablespoons water

Combine flours. Beat eggs and water in separate bowl and add 3/4 cup flour mixture. Mix well, then mix in remaining flour. Roll thin, let air dry 20 minutes. Roll up and cut desired thickness or use a pasta maker. Boil water and cook 2-3 minutes, or air dry and store in an airtight container.

Pita Pockets

- 1 tablespoon yeast
- 2 cups water
- 4 cups wheat flour
- 1 teaspoon salt

Dissolve yeast in water. Add 2 cups flour and beat until smooth. Add salt and remaining flour. Knead until smooth, about 10 minutes. Let rest 15 minutes. Cut into 8 equal pieces and lightly roll into patties 1/4 inch thick. Transfer to floured wax paper and let rest 45 minutes. Preheat oven to 500°. Peel patties off wax paper and transfer to ungreased cookie sheet and place in oven. Do not open oven for 4 minutes, then flip patties and bake 1-4 minutes longer but do not brown. Cut pockets in half and separate sides. Makes 8 whole pitas.

> "...let (men) be sparing of the life of animals; it is pleasing saith the Lord that flesh be used only in times of famine — and why to be used in famine? Because domesticated animals would naturally die, and may as well be made use of by man."
>
> *Hyrum Smith, 1842*

Wheat Tortillas

- ◆ 5 cups wheat flour
- ◆ 1 tablespoon salt
- ◆ 1/2 teaspoon baking powder
- ◆ 3/4 cup olive oil
- ◆ 1 2/3 cups hot water

Sift flour, salt and baking powder together in a large bowl. Add oil and water and knead until smooth. Divide into 4 parts. Cover 3 divided parts until ready to use. Divide each part into 6 balls. Roll each ball of dough flat on a lightly floured surface from the center outward as thin as possible without tearing. Put in a lightly oiled hot skillet for 20 seconds each side, pressing tortilla with a clean dishcloth – this helps the tortilla get light and bubble up. Freeze tortillas if not eaten within 2 days. Makes 2 dozen.

Butter

Mixer or Blender method

- ◆ cream or whipping cream

Use any amount of cream or whipping cream. Bring to 60° in mixing bowl. Beat at medium speed until cream separates into clumps of butter the size of wheat berries or larger. If cream whips before forming butter, continue to beat until it breaks. Drain off the buttermilk and rinse under cold water. Press with a wooden spoon or cold fingers to remove excess liquid. Add 1/2 teaspoon salt to every 1/2 lb butter. May churn small quantities of cream in the blender at lowest speed. Refrigerate or freeze.

Butter Substitute

Highly Nutritious
♦ Flax Seed Meal (Ground Flax Seed)
Substitute flax seed meal for butter, shortening or oil at a ratio of
3 to 1 in baking foods. For example: 1 1/2 cup flax seed meal
can replace 1/2 cup butter in a recipe.

Mayonnaise

♦ 2 eggs, room temperature
♦ 2 tablespoons lemon juice
♦ 1/4 teaspoon salt
♦ 1 teaspoon dry mustard
♦ 1/4 cup oil
♦ 1 tablespoon parsley (optional)
♦ 1 teaspoon dill weed (optional)
♦ 1/2 teaspoon paprika (optional)
♦ 1-2 tablespoons honey (optional)

Combine eggs, lemon juice, salt and mustard in a blender at high
speed for 1 minute. Add oil gradually, processing until mixture
thickens. Add any optional ingredients and blend. Refrigerate in
non-metal container. Yields 15oz.

Catsup

♦ 2 cups pureed tomatoes
♦ 1 teaspoon salt
♦ 1/4 cup cider vinegar or lemon juice
♦ 2 tablespoons honey
♦ 1/4 teaspoon garlic powder (optional)
♦ 1/4 teaspoon basil (optional)
♦ 1/4 teaspoon nutmeg (optional)
♦ 1/4 teaspoon dry mustard (optional)

Combine all ingredients in blender or with a wire whisk. Simmer in
a saucepan for 5 minutes. Store uncovered in the refrigerator.
Yields 2 1/2 cups.

Chinese Barbeque Sauce

- ◆ 1/2 cup honey
- ◆ 1 cup catsup
- ◆ 1/2 cup soy sauce
- ◆ 4 minced garlic cloves

Combine all ingredients in a bowl and store covered in refrigerator.

Hummus

Bean dip/spread

- ◆ 2 cups cooked garbanzo beans, drained, reserving cooking liquid
- ◆ 1 minced garlic clove
- ◆ 2-4 tablespoons tahini or smooth
- ◆ peanut butter
- ◆ juice of 1/2 lemon
- ◆ 1 tablespoon oil

Process all ingredients in food processor, blender or mortar and pestle until smooth, thinning with reserved bean liquid as desired. Yields 24oz.

Refried Beans

- ◆ 3 cups cooked pinto beans
- ◆ 1/4 cup chopped onions
- ◆ 2 minced garlic cloves
- ◆ 2 tablespoons olive oil
- ◆ 1 teaspoon cumin

Sauté onion and garlic in oil until clear. Mash half the beans and add to onion and garlic, sauté 10 minutes. Add cumin and remaining beans. Water may be added to keep desired consistency.

Peanut Butter

♦ 1 lb. raw shelled peanuts

Place peanuts in a single layer on a shallow cookie sheet and roast at 325° for 10 to 40 minutes until roasted to the taste. This is an optional step. Pour peanuts into a food processor and process until smooth. If using a blender, pour only 1/4 cup peanuts and process until butter begins to form around blades, then add 2 tablespoons peanuts at a time, but DO NOT scrape butter away from the blades. Remove butter after having processed about one cup and repeat the process.

Nut Butters

♦ 2 cups almonds or any preferred nut
♦ 1/8 teaspoon salt
♦ 1/2 cup milk or milk alternative

Put nuts in a single layer on a cookie sheet in the oven at 350° for 8 minutes. This is an optional step. In a food processor grind the nuts to a fine powder and add the milk while still processing until smooth.

"There is...an indifference even among us that are not found among many well-informed people in the world. Their old traditions cling to them...Pestilence(s) of various kinds which we are led to expect through the word of the Lord are yet to break through, and will have their effect in calling the Saints' attention to those laws of life and health."

Apostle George Q. Cannon, 1867

Soymilk

- ◆ 2/3 cups dry soybeans
- ◆ 4 cups water
- ◆ 3/4 cup oil
- ◆ 1/4 teaspoon salt
- ◆ 1/4 cup honey

Soak soybeans for 12 hours or overnight. Drain and add enough water to the soaking water to measure 4 cups. Grind soaked soybeans and 2 cups of the water with a fine blade in food processor or blender at low speed for 3 minutes. Put soybean mixture into the top of a double boiler and add remaining 2 cups water and cook over boiling water for 30 minutes. Strain through a cheesecloth. Rinse out top of double boiler and return strained soymilk to it. Cook 30 more minutes over boiling water, strain through cheesecloth again. Pour 2/3 cup hot soymilk into a blender or processor, add oil, and blend on medium low for five minutes, no less. Add remaining soymilk, salt, honey and blend for 2 minutes longer. Refrigerate. Will keep for 1 week. Yields one quart.

Cashew Milk

- ◆ 1 cup raw cashews
- ◆ 4 cups water
- ◆ honey to taste, optional

Combine nuts, water and honey in a food processsor or blender and process on high 2 minutes. Refrigerate. Cashew milk is naturally sweet, so you may want to try it before adding honey. Yields 4 cups.

Sesame Milk

- ◆ 3/4 cup sesame seeds
- ◆ 4 cups water
- ◆ 2-4 tablespoons honey, optional

Combine seeds, water and honey in blender or food processor on high for 2 minutes. Strain and refrigerate. Yields 4 cups.

Diastatic Malt

White sugar alternative.
- ◆ 1 cup wheat berry sprouts
- ◆ tepid water

Spread sprouts on ungreased cookie sheet and dry in the oven at 150° for 8 hours or until sprouts are crunchy. Grind in food mill or blender. Store in refrigerator in an air-tight container. Will keep indefinitely.

Date Sugar

Fantastic white sugar alternative.
- ◆ dates

Pit and dry dates completely, then grind them in a processor and dry again. That's your date sugar!

Wheat Crepes

Also known as Swedish pancakes.
- ◆ 1 1/2 cup milk or alternative
- ◆ 3 eggs
- ◆ 1 cup wheat flour
- ◆ butter

Process milk and eggs in a blender, processor or with a whisk. Add flour and blend until smooth. Coat small skillet with 1 teaspoon butter and heat until smoking. Pour about 3 table-spoons batter into the skillet and swirl around until it is a small tortilla size and cook 1 minute until browned. Loosen edges and flip, cook 30 seconds more. Repeat until batter is gone. Goes fast if you have 3 or 4 skillets going at once.

Buckwheat Crepes

- ◆ 3 eggs
- ◆ 1/2 cup milk or alternative
- ◆ 3/4 cup yogurt (6 oz.)
- ◆ 1/2 cup buckwheat flour
- ◆ 1/4 cup wheat flour
- ◆ 1 tablespoon melted butter

Beat eggs until thick and add milk. Sift flours and blend with egg-milk mixture. Stir in butter. Let stand 1 hour before using. Refer to wheat crepe recipe for cooking instructions.

Rice or Grain Crust

Useful for pizza or quiche.

- ◆ 3 cups cooked rice or grains
- ◆ 2 beaten eggs
- ◆ 1 cup shredded mozzerella cheese

Combine all ingredients, mix well. Press into a greased pizza or pie plate. Bake at 450° for 20 minutes.

Easy Oil Crust

- ◆ 2 cups wheat flour
- ◆ 1/2 cup oil
- ◆ 1/4 cup cold water
- ◆ salt to taste

Mix flour and salt. Combine oil and water separately and add flour, mix with fork. Shape with hands into 2 balls. Let stand covered for 5 minutes. Roll out between 2 sheets of waxed paper. Fit into 10 inch pie plate, prick with fork and bake at 375° for 10 to 12 minutes, repeat with other ball.

21

No Cream Soup Base

- ◆ 6 cups boiling water
- ◆ 1 cup white bean flour (ground in grinder or food processor)
- ◆ 2 tablespoons multi-seasnoning blend, optional but recommended

Whisk bean flour into boiling water and add seasonings. Stir and cook 3 to 5 minutes. Add to soups or means to "cream" them. Makes 6 cups.

No Cream Soup Base II

- ◆ 3 cups stock
- ◆ 1/2 cup rolled oats

Boil stock and add oats. Simmer covered for 1 hour. Purée in blender. Add to soups or meals to "cream" them.

Wonton Skins or Egg Roll Wrappers

- ◆ 1 egg
- ◆ 2 tablespoons water
- ◆ 1 1/2 tablespoons oil
- ◆ 1 teaspoon salt
- ◆ 1 cup wheat flour

Combine ingredients to form a smooth ball. On a floured surface roll out almost transparent thin. Cut with pizza wheel. Makes 2 dozen 3 x 3 skins or 1 dozen egg roll wrappers.

Wheat Things

- ◆ 2 1/4 cup wheat flour
- ◆ 1/2 cup wheat grain
- ◆ 1 1/4 teaspoon salt
- ◆ 3/4 cup oil
- ◆ 3/4 cup water

Combine flour, wheat germ and salt in large mixing bowl. Add oil and water and knead until smooth. Roll out sheet very thin on a lightly floured flat cookie sheet. Cut into 1 1/2 inch squares with pizza cutter. Prick each with a fork and lightly salt. Bake at 350° for 7 to 10 minutes. If crackers aren't crisp when cooked, return to turned off oven and let sit until crisp. Maks 10 dozen crackers.

Herbed Wheat Things

- ◆ 1 teaspoon parsely flakes
- ◆ 1 teaspoon dill weed
- ◆ 1 teaspoon onion powder

Add herbs to dry ingredients and follow steps listed.

Soda Crackers

- ◆ 2 cups wheat pastry flour (pastry makes crispier crackers)
- ◆ 1 teaspoon salt
- ◆ 1/2 teaspoon baking soda
- ◆ 1/4 cup softened butter
- ◆ 1/2 cup buttermilk (or 1/2 cup milk or alternative + 2 teaspoons lemon juice)
- ◆ 1 egg

Combine flour, salt and soda in a bowl. Cut in butter and mix until crumbly. Add milk and egg, stirring until dough forms. Add more flour for desired consistency. Roll out 1/8 inch thick on floured surface. Use pizza cutter to cut into squares and place on a lightly oiled cookie sheet. Prick with fork, sprinkle with salt, bake at 400° until browned. Makes about 30 crackers.

Wheat Nuts

- ◆ wheat berries
- ◆ oil
- ◆ salt and preferred seasonings

Soak wheat overnight, then boil for 30 minutes. Drain and remove excess water by rolling berries in a paper towel. Heat oil in a pot until it "pops" when water is sprinkled on it. Put half of the berries in a strainer and deep fry for 1 1/2 minutes. Drain on paper towels and salt.

Graham Crackers

- ◆ 2 cups wheat flour
- ◆ 1 cup wheat germ
- ◆ 1 teaspoon baking powder
- ◆ 1/2 teaspoon salt
- ◆ 1/2 cup softened butter
- ◆ 3/4 cup milk or alternative
- ◆ 1/2 cup honey
- ◆ 1 teaspoon molasses

Mix flour, wheat germ, baking powder, and salt in large bowl. Stir in remaining ingredients and mix together to form a ball. Add flour if dough is sticky. Roll dough 1/8 inch thick on a floured surface. Cut with pizza cutter into 3 x 3 squares. Place on cookie sheet and prick with fork. Bake at 325° for 12 to 15 minutes. Makes 3 dozen crackers.

Graham Cracker Pie Crust

- ◆ 2/3 cups graham cracker crumbs
- ◆ 1/4 cup wheat germ
- ◆ 1/2 teaspoon cinnamon
- ◆ 3/4 cup melted butter
- ◆ 1 tablespoon honey, maple syrup, or molasses

Combine crumbs, germ and cinnamon. Add the butter, then honey. Press into a greased pie plate. Bake at 300° for 10 minutes.

Bean Puree

Butter, oil and shortening alternative.
+ I cup dried beans
+ I teaspoon salt

Soak beans overnight, drain and cover, add salt. Boil enough water to cover beans and simmer covered until beans are tender *or* let beans soak for 2 more days or so, changing the water once every 24 hours. Separate beans from liquid. Add only enough liquid back to blend the beans into purée consistency. Process in a blender or food processor. Makes 2 cups, can be frozen.

Pesto Sauce

+ I tablespoon pine nuts
+ 6 tablespoons olive oil
+ 3 minced garlic cloves
+ 6 tablespoons chopped fresh basil
+ I tablespoon chopped fresh parsely
+ salt to taste

Combine ingredients in a blender or processor and puree. Yields 3/4 cup.

Apple Butter

+ applesauce

Cook applesauce on low heat in a crock pot or oven until applesauce is thickened. To test, place a spoonful on a plate. It is done when no watery ring forms around the edge of the applesauce.

Applesauce

♦ 4 apples, peeled and chopped
♦ I cup water
♦ I/2 teaspoon cinnamon
♦ I/2 teaspoon nutmeg (optional)

Bring all ingredients to a boil in covered I quart saucepan. Simmer uncovered for I5 minutes, stirring often to break up apple chunks. Remove and process in blender or processor until smooth. Yields 2 to 3 cups.

Natural Dyes

Ideal for Easter eggs or dying fabric.

♦ Yellow: yellow onion skins, turmeric, chamomile flowers, sage, or celery leaves
♦ Orange: yellow ingredients plus some beet juice
♦ Red: beets, safflower seeds, paprika, rose hips tea
♦ Blue: blueberries, grape juice concentrate, red cabbage
♦ Brown: black tea, white oak, juniper berries, coffee beans, barberry
♦ Purple: blackberries, grapes, violets
♦ Green: alfalfa, spinach, kale, tansy, nettle, chervil, sorrel, parsely, carrot or beat tops
♦ Khaki: red onion skins

Hard cook eggs or boil fabric with I tablespoon or more white vinegar. Place dying items in non-aluminum pots, cover with water and boil 5 or more minutes to extract the color. Some things, like grapes, may take longer than an hour. Crush ingredients as they boil to extract as much as possible and strain when done. Most dyes should be used hot. Leave egg or fabric in the dyed water until it reaches the desired color.

Year Round Breakfasts

Year Round Breakfast Staples

- ◆ Sweetened grain cereals, ie oats, wheat, barley, spelt, millet
- ◆ Muffins and breads
- ◆ French toast
- ◆ Pancakes and waffles
- ◆ In season fruit

Common sense says that whole grain based foods and seasonal fruits should be for breakfast. They're great tasting, high in energy, raise your blood sugar slowly and naturally and maintain it there for a while, and are extremely filling. Plus, they will act as a gentle laxative to help start your day.

Granola

- ◆ 4 cups rolled oats
- ◆ I cup coconut shreds, optional
- ◆ I cup wheat germ
- ◆ I/2 cup oil
- ◆ 3/4 cup honey
- ◆ I teaspoon vanilla
- ◆ I/4 cup sunflower seeds, optional
- ◆ 3/4 cup raisings, optional
- ◆ I/4 cup chopped almonds
- ◆ I/4 cup sesame seeds, optional

Combine oats, germ, oil, honey and vanilla in a bowl. Spread on a cookie sheet and bake at 300° for 20 minutes, stirring every 5 minutes. Remove and add almonds and optional items.

> "Fruits (and vegetables) should be eaten raw, fully ripe, and 'in the season thereof'...in liberal amounts by young and old,...grain should form the bulk of the human dietary."
> *Apostle John A Widstoe, 1950*

Peanut Butter Granola

- 2 3/4 cups rolled oats
- 1/4 cup wheat germ
- 1/4 cup sunflower seeds
- 2 tablespoons oil
- 1/4 cup honey
- 1 teaspoon vanilla
- 3/4 cup peanut butter
- 1/2 cup raisins, optional

Combine oats, germ and seeds in bowl. Heat oil and honey in a saucepan over medium heat, stirring constantly. Remove and add vanilla and peanut butter, blending well. Pour over dry mixture and mix with a wooden spoon and spread onto a cookie sheet. Bake at 225° for 1 hour or at 300° for 30 to 40 minutes. Remove and add raisings. Yields 4 cups.

Blender Pancakes or Waffles

So easy and nutritious! Jones family favorite.

- 1 1/4 cup water
- 1 cup wheat berries
- 1 egg
- 2 tablespoons oil
- 1 tablespoon honey or maple syrup
- 1/2 teaspoon salt
- 1 tablespoon baking powder

Combine water and wheat in a blender on high for 3 minutes. Add egg, oil, honey, and salt and blend 20 seconds. Add baking powder and pulse 3 times, just enough to mix. Mixture should foam up and get very light. Cook as usual.

Multi Grain Variation

- 3/4 cup any grain or bean mixture
- 1/4 cup wheat berries
- Additional ingredients listed above

Follow above instructions.

Grain Muffins

- ◆ 2 cups wheat flour
- ◆ I teaspoon baking soda
- ◆ 1/4 cup honey
- ◆ I teaspoon cinnamon
- ◆ 1/2 teaspoon salt
- ◆ I egg
- ◆ I cup buttermilk, yogurt, or sour milk
- ◆ 3 tablespoons oil

Mix dry ingredients in a bowl. Make a well in the center and add buttermilk, egg and oil and stir until moist. Fill greased muffin cups 1/2 full and bake at 375° for 15 minutes.

Millet Breakfast Cereal

- ◆ I cup millet
- ◆ I teaspoon salt
- ◆ I qt. water
- ◆ honey and milk
- ◆ in season fruit, optional

Boil water and add millet. Simmer covered on low heat for 45 minutes. Add fruit and cook additional 15 minutes. Serve with honey and milk.

Mixed Grain Cereal

- ◆ I cup rolled oats
- ◆ I cup cracked wheat
- ◆ I cup pearled barley
- ◆ 1/2 cup millet
- ◆ I cup sunflower seeds, optional
- ◆ I cup raisins, optional

Combine all ingredients and store in air-tight container. Makes 5 1/2 cup mix. To make 4 servings: Bring 1 3/4 cup water to boil, add 3/4 cup cereal mix. Simmer covered 15 minutes or until softened. Sweeten.

Fruit Syrups

- ♦ 1 teaspoon cornstarch or flour
- ♦ 1 cup 100% fruit juice, not from concentrate
- ♦ 1 teaspoon honey

Combine ingredients in a saucepan and boil until thickened.
Serves 4.

Muesli

- ♦ 1 cup rolled oats
- ♦ 1/2 cup rolled spelt*
- ♦ 1/2 cup rolled triticale*
- ♦ 2 cups rolled kamut or barley*
- ♦ 1/4 cup chopped dates
- ♦ 1/4 cup raisins
- ♦ 1 dried pear, chopping and tossed in flour
- ♦ 1/4 cup almonds
- ♦ 8 raw filberts
- ♦ 4 pecans

*If you cannot find this, just substitute with rolled oats.
Combine filberts, pecans and almonds in a blender and pulse to
a powder. Then combine all ingredients in an airtight container.
Serve with milk or alternative. Yields 4 cups.

"The foods used by many careless or uninformed modern
people yeild a shortage...of many necessary food factors,
especially of vitamins and minerals...because so much of
the food so-called civilized man today is preserved,
salted, sugared, purified, polished, pickled, canned,
extracted, concentrated, heated, dried, frozen, thawed,
stored, packaged, processed, and refined!...The Word of
Wisdom warns against the 'evils and designs which do and
will exist in the hearts of conspiring men in the last days.'"

Apostle J. A. Widtsoe, 1950

Year Round Lunches

Lentil Salad

- ◆ I cup dry lentils
- ◆ I qt. water
- ◆ I teaspoon salt
- ◆ 3/4 cup oil
- ◆ 1/4 cup vinegar
- ◆ 1/2 teaspoon salt
- ◆ 1/2 teaspoon dry mustard
- ◆ 1/2 teaspoon paprika
- ◆ 1/8 teaspoon pepper
- ◆ 1/4 cup sweet relish
- ◆ 1/4 cup chopped onion

Boil water and salt, add lentils and simmer covered 20 to 30 minutes. Drain and combine remaining ingredients with lentils. Refrigerate at least 2 hours. Serves 6.

Un Meatballs

- ◆ I 1/2 cup breadcrumbs
- ◆ I cup cheddar cheese
- ◆ 1/2 cup minced walnuts
- ◆ 4-6 beaten eggs, seasonally adjusted
- ◆ 1/2 cup chopped onions
- ◆ I minced garlic clove
- ◆ 1/2 teaspoon salt
- ◆ oil for browning
- ◆ 4 cups preferred sauce for un meatballs

Combine breadcrumbs, 1/2 cup cheese, nuts, eggs, onion, garlic and salt. Shape by tablespoonfuls into balls. Brown in heated oil and drain. Place in 2 qt. casserole and top with sauce. Bake at 375° for 30 minutes, top with remaining cheese and bake 10 minutes longer. Serves 6.

31

Potato-Less Salad

- ◆ 2 cups cooked wheat berries
- ◆ 1 minced onion
- ◆ 2 teaspoons mustard
- ◆ 3/4 cup mayonnaise (see recipe)
- ◆ 3 chopped hard-boiled eggs, seasonally optional

Combine and chill. Serves 4.

Wheat Loaf

- ◆ 2 cups cooked wheat berries
- ◆ 2 cups no cream soup base (see recipe)
- ◆ 1 cup seasonal vegetable, ie peas, carrots, corn
- ◆ 1 teaspoon salt
- ◆ 1 tablespoon softened butter
- ◆ 1 cup sliced mushrooms
- ◆ 1 cup breadcrumbs

Combine ingredients in order given, except breadcrumbs. Place in caserole dish and cover with breadcrums. Bake at 350° for 40 minutes. Serves 4 to 6.

Garbanzo and Peanut Soup

- ◆ 1 1/2 cup dry garbanzo beans, soaked overnight
- ◆ 1 tablespoon olive oil
- ◆ 3 minced garlic cloves
- ◆ 1 minced onion
- ◆ 6 cups stock or water
- ◆ 2 tablespoons soy sauce
- ◆ 1/4 cup chopped peanuts
- ◆ 1/4 cup minced parsely or cilantro

Heat oil in stock pot on medium high, sauté garlic and onion 4 minutes. Add soaked garbanzos, stock, soy sauce and simmer covered 3 hours, or heat in crock pot on high. Purée soup in blender or processor, serve topped with peanuts and parsley or cilantro. Easy to freeze. Serves 4 to 6.

Vinaigrette Dressing

- ◆ 1/4 cup light oil
- ◆ 1/4 cup white wine vinegar
- ◆ 1 minced garlic clove
- ◆ 1 tablespoon mustard
- ◆ 3 tablespoons fresh minced oregano
- ◆ salt and pepper to taste

Combine all ingredients. makes 1 1/4 cups.

Orange Salad Dressing

- ◆ 1 cup orange juice
- ◆ 1/2 cup water
- ◆ 2 cups sunflower seeds, soaked 8 to 12 hours
- ◆ juice of 2 lemons, seasonally optional
- ◆ 4 tablespoons almost butter
- ◆ 2 teaspoons salt
- ◆ 4 green onions
- ◆ 2 teaspoons curry powder

Combine all ingredients in blender or food processor and purée until smooth. Yields 2 cups.

33

Year Round Dinners

Baked Bean Casserole

Jones Family Favorite.

- 1 cup chopped onion
- 1/2 cup catsup
- 1 teaspoon salt
- 1/2 - 3/4 cup honey
- 1 teaspoon mustard
- 8 cups any cooked bean combination (kidney, pinto, etc. – equals 4 cans of beans)
- 1/2 lb. crumbled and cooked bacon, seasonally optional
- 1/2 lb cooked hamburger, seasonally optional
- 1/2 cup diced green pepper, seasonally optional

Brown onion, pepper and meats. Add remaining ingredients and transfer to a glass bowl. Bake at 350° for 30 minutes. Serve over cooked rice or grain. Serves 8.

"We are part of life and should study carefully our relationship to it. We should be in sympathy with it, and not allow our prejudices to create a desire for its destruction...The unnecessary destruction of life is a distinct spiritual loss to the human family....(The love of life) exalts the spiritual nature of those in need of divine favor...Love of nature is akin to the love of God; the two are inseparable."

President Joseph F. Smith, 1913

Barley and Almond Casserole

Jones Family Favorite.

- 2 tablespoons butter
- 3/4 cup slivered almonds
- 1/4 cup butter
- 1 cup barley
- 1 chopped onion
- 1/4 teaspoon pepper
- 1/4 teaspoon salt

- 1 3/4 cup stock
- 1 cup minced chives or green onion, seasonally optional
- 1/2 cup minced parsely, seasonally optional

Heat 2 tablespoons butter, add almonds and toast, set aside. Melt 1/4 cup butter and add barley and onion, sauté until tender and remove. Add almonds, parsely, chives, salt and pepper. Spoon into 1 1/2 qt casserole dish. Boil stock and pour on barley mixture. Bake at 375° for 1 hour.

Optional White Sauce

- 2 cups milk or alternative
- 4 tablespoons wheat flour
- 4 tablespoons butter

Whisk milk and flour until blended, add butter and bring to a boil. Simmer 5 minutes until thickened. Add to barley dish. May substitute the no-cream soup base.

Kasha Varniskas

- 1 beaten egg
- 3/4 cup cooked kasha
- 2 tablespoons oil
- 1 cup chopped onion

- 1 1/2 cup stock
- dash of pepper
- 1 cup uncooked pasta

Combine egg and kasha in small bowl. Stir this mixture in a large, dry skillet over medium heat, stirring constantly until egg has cooked and grains are separated, remove. Heat oil in 2 qt. saucepan and sauté onion 4 minutes. Add kasha mixture, stock and pepper, then bring to boil. Simmer covered 15 minutes. Meanwhile cook pasta, then combine with akasha. Serves 4.

Quinoa Eggdrop Soup

- 1 3/4 cup stock
- 1 1/2 cup + 2 tablespoons water, divided
- 1/4 cup cooked quinoa
- 1 tablespoon flour
- 2 eggs
- 2 tablespoons minced scallions

Boil stock and 1 1/2 cup water and add quinoa, simmer covered 20 minutes. Meanwhile combine flour and 2 tablespoons water in a small bowl, add to stock. In the same small bowl, beat the egg and add to boiling soup, stirring in one direction until egg is cooked. Remove from heat and add scallion. Serves 6.

Fried Rice

- 2 cups minced onions
- 1 minced garlic clove
- 2 tablespoons oil
- 4 beaten eggs
- 3 cups cooked brown rice
- 4 thinly sliced green onions
- 1 1/2 cup chopped cooked meat, seasonally optional or mushrooms or tofu
- 1 cup bean sprouts, optional
- 3 tablespoons soy sauce
- 1 1/2 cup chopped, steamed seasonal vegetables

Heat oil in large skillet or wok and sauté onions and garlic 3 minutes. Push to one side, add more oil if necessary and add eggs. Scramble and cook until firm. Add rice, green onions, meat, sprouts, soy sauce and vegetables. Serves 8.

Couscous
or Quinoa and Lentils

- ♦ 1/2 stick of cinnamon
- ♦ 6 whole cloves
- ♦ 2 tablespoons oil
- ♦ 1/2 cup chopped onion
- ♦ 1 minced garlic clove
- ♦ 2 1/4 cup water
- ♦ 1/2 teaspoon salt
- ♦ 1/2 cup cooked lentils
- ♦ 1/2 cup currants or raisins
- ♦ 2 tablespoons chopped fresh parsley
- ♦ 2 tablespoons butter

Wrap cinnamon and cloves in cheesecloth or pantyhose and tie top with string. Heat oil in 2 qt. saucepan and sauté onions and garlic 4 minutes. Add water and salt, then bring to boil. Add lentils and spice sack, simmer 50 minutes. Add couscous or quinoa and simmer 3 minutes more. Remove and let stand 5 minutes. Discard spice pack. Stir in currant, parsley and butter. Serves 4-6

WheatBurger

- ♦ 1 cup wheat berries
- ♦ 2 cups water
- ♦ 2 cups any variety cooked beans
- ♦ 1 egg
- ♦ salt and pepper to taste

Soak wheat berries overnight. Boil water and add wheat, cook 1 hour. Blend wheat in blender and add beans. While blending add egg, salt and pepper. Mold into patties and fry in skillet or crumble and fry like ground meat.

Year Round Sides and Breads

Bagels

- ♦ 2 tablespoons yeast
- ♦ 2 cups warm water
- ♦ 1 teaspoon salt
- ♦ 2 tablespoons honey
- ♦ 3 cups wheat flour

Dissolve yeast and honey in water. Add flour and salt, mix until firm and not sticky. Let raise until doubled, then form rings. Let rings raise 15 minutes, then boil 3 minutes each, turning often. Bake at 425° for 25 minutes.

Challah Bread

Jewish Sabbath Bread.

- ♦ 2 tablespoons yeast
- ♦ 2 cups warm water
- ♦ 2-3 eggs
- ♦ 1/2 cup honey
- ♦ 2 teaspoons salt
- ♦ 2 tablespoons butter or oil, may need more
- ♦ 7-8 cups wheat flour
- ♦ egg wash (recipe follows)

Dissolve yeast in water in a bowl. Add eggs, honey, salt, butter and 3 1/2 cup flour. Beat well and add remaining flour to make a soft dough. Knead 5-10 minutes, adding more flour if necessary. Use as little flour as possible to create a delicate challah. It should be velvety soft. Let rise 1 1/2 - 2 hours or until doubled. Punch down, let rise again. Shape into two twisted or braided loaves, place on ungreased cookie sheets and let rise again. Brush with egg wash. Bake at 350° for 35 to 40 minutes until browned.

Egg Wash

- ♦ 1 egg
- ♦ 1 tablespoon water

Combine and beat with fork.

Sprouted Wheat Bread

◆ 2 tablespoons yeast
◆ 2 cups warm water
◆ 3/4 cup molasses or honey
◆ 6-7 c. wheat flour
◆ 2 teaspoons salt
◆ 1/4 cup oil
◆ 2 cups sprouted wheat
◆ 2 eggs, optional
◆ 2 cups rolled oats, optional

Dissolve yeast and honey in water. Stir in 3 1/2 cup flour to make a sponge. Add salt, oil, sprouted wheat and optional ingredients. Add enough remaining flour to make a stiff dough. Knead 8 minutes. Let dough rise until doubled. Divide dough into halves and place in greased loaf pans and let rise until doubled. Bake at 400° for 10 minutes. Reduce to 375° and bake 30 more minutes.

Harvest Bread

◆ 2 cups wheat berries or any grain
◆ 1 tablespoon yeast
◆ 2 1/4 cup warm water
◆ 1/4 cup honey
◆ 1/2 cup cornmeal
◆ 1 cup rolled oats
◆ 4 1/2 cup wheat flour
◆ 2 tablespoons butter
◆ 1 1/2 teaspoon salt

Soak wheat berries overnight and cook in abundant water for 1 hour, reserving leftover liquid. Dissolve yeast in 1/4 cup warm water. Add to wheat in large bowl with 3/4 cup soaking water, honey, cornmeal oats, 1/2 cup flour, butter and salt. Combine and then stir in remaining flour and knead 10 minutes. Let rise until doubled. Punch down and let rise again. Divide into 2 loaves and place in greased loaf pans. Let rise until doubled. Bake at 350° for 35 to 40 minutes. Brush with melted butter.

Hamburger Buns

Fast and versatile.

- ◆ 4 cups wheat flour
- ◆ 2 tablespoons yeast
- ◆ I cup milk or alternative
- ◆ 3/4 cup water
- ◆ I/2 cup oil
- ◆ 4 tablespoons honey
- ◆ I teaspoon salt

Combine 2 cups flour and yeast in large bowl. Heat milk, water, oil, honey and salt in saucepan to 120-130°—very warm but not scalding. Pour into flour mixture and beat 3 minutes or 300 strokes. Add enough remaining flour to make a soft dough. Knead briefly. Let rise 10 minutes. Pull out a scoop of dough to form a bun, flattening between palms or rolling out to 1/2 inch thick, and cut with jar ring or equivelant. Repeat with remaining dough and let rise on greased baking sheet for 1/2 hour. Bake at 400° for 12 to 15 minutes. Yields 15 bun pairs. Recipe may be used for hot dog buns, pizza dough, dinner rolls, soft pretzels, cinnamon rolls and bread loaves.

"The fathers and mothers have laid the foundation for many of these diseases...until the people are reduced to their present condition. The people have laid the foundation of short life through their diet...with improper motives, and at improper times. I would be glad to tell mothers how to lay the foundation of health in their children...Latter-Day Saints who live merely to get ready to die are not worth much; rather get ready to live to the Glory of your Father in Heaven and to do the work He has given you to do."

President Brigham Young, 1855

English Muffins

- 4 cups wheat flour
- 1 teaspoon salt
- 1 tablespoon yeast
- 1/2 cup warm milk or alternative
- 1 cup warm water
- 3 tablespoons diastatic malt, sucanat, or date sugar
- 1/4 c, softened butter
- cornmeal

Sift flour and salt together. Combine yeast and warm milk and rest 5 minutes. Add water and "sugar." Work in 2 cups flour mixture and let stand 1 1/2 hours. Beat in softened butter and remaining flour. Pat dough on lightly cornmeal dusted board. Cover and let rise. Roll out dough to 1/2 inch thick and cut muffins with jar ring or equivelant. Let stand 20 minutes. Heat lightly oiled skillet, fry each side 5 to 7 minutes.

Oven Baked English Muffins

- omit 1/2 cup water
- add 2/3 cup yogurt to above recipe

Sprinkle tops of muffins with cornmeal and place on baking sheet instead of skillet. Place another baking sheet on top. Let rise 30 minutes. Bake at 375° for 15 minutes.

Crescent Rolls

- 4 tsp. yeast
- I cup warm water
- I teaspoon honey
- I cup oil
- 3 tablespoons honey
- 2 teaspoons salt
- I cup boiling water
- 2 beaten eggs
- 6 cups wheat flour
- 1/2 teaspoon water
- 4 tablespoons toasted sesame seeds, optional
- I beaten egg + 1/2 teaspoon water

Dissolve yeast in I cup warm water, add I teaspoon honey in large bowl, combine oil, I tablespoon honey, salt and boiling water. When lukewarm, add eggs and the dissolved yeast. Gradually add the flour, but do not knead. Refrigerate until firm. Divide into thirds and roll each onto floured surface in a large circle, as thin as possible. Brush with beaten egg/water solution. Sprinkle sesame seeds over surface. Cut each circle into triangular wedges, about 2 inches wide at outside edge. Roll up each wedge towards the point, lift off of surface, dip top into egg mixture, then in sesame seeds. Place on greased cookie sheet, leaving enough room for each roll to rise. Let rise 1 1/2 hours. Bake at 425° for 25 minutes. Yields 4 dozen.

Lima Bean Side Dish

Every kid's dream, right?
- 2 cups cooked lima beans
- I tablespoon chervil
- 1/2 tablespoons rosemary
- 1/2 teaspoon sage
- dash of onion powder
- I tablespoon oil
- diced tomato, seasonally optional

Combine all ingredients and warm through. Top with tomato.

Boston Baked Beans

- ◆ 3 cups cooked navy beans
- ◆ 1 chopped onion
- ◆ 1 tablespoon oil
- ◆ 1/2 cup molasses, maple syrup, or honey
- ◆ 4 tablespoons soy sauce
- ◆ 1 tablespoon mustard

Combine ingredients and bake at 325° for 45 minutes. May also be used as a main dish, served over cooked rice or grains.

Toasted Millet

- ◆ 1 cup uncooked millet
- ◆ 2 teaspoons sesame or olive oil
- ◆ 1/2 teaspoon cumin
- ◆ 1/4 teaspoon dry mustard
- ◆ 1 chopped onion
- ◆ 3 cups stock

Heat oil, add millet and spices and sauté 10 minutes. Add stock and simmer covered on low heat for 15 minutes.

Chili Nuts

- ◆ 1 egg white
- ◆ 3/4 lb. seasonal unsalted nut, preferably cashew
- ◆ 2 teaspoons coarse salt
- ◆ 1 teaspoon crushed red pepper flakes
- ◆ 1/2 teaspoon cumin
- ◆ 1/2 teaspoon oregano
- ◆ 1/4 teaspoon ground hot red pepper

Beat egg white, then add nuts and toss. Combine the herbs and toss with nuts. Spread nuts on a greased cookie sheet and bake at 300° for 25 minutes, stirring 2 to 3 times. Serves 12.

Year Round Desserts

Rob Roy Cookies

- 1 cup butter
- 3/4 cup honey
- 1 teaspoon salt
- 1/2 teaspoon cloves
- 2 eggs
- 2 tablespoons buttermilk or alternative
- 2 1/2 cups wheat flour
- 3/4 teaspoon baking soda
- 2 cups rolled oats
- 1 cup chopped nuts, optional
- 1 cup raisins, optional

Combine all ingredients and place by the spoonfuls on a greased cookie sheet. Bake at 375° for 10 to 12 minutes.

Wheat Cake

Light and fluffy.

- 1 cup honey
- 1 cup softened butter
- 2 teaspoons vanilla
- 3 eggs
- 3 cups wheat flour
- 1 tablespoon + 1 teaspoon baking powder
- 1/2 teaspoon salt
- 3/4 cup milk or alternative

Beat honey and butter in a large bowl until fluffy. Add vanilla and eggs. Mix flour, baking powder and salt in a small bowl, add to honey and butter mixture alternately with the milk. Beat on high 2 minutes or 200 strokes. Pour into 9 x 13 cake pan that's been oiled only. Bake at 350° for 35 minutes or until toothpick comes out clean. Serve with cake or fruit toppings.

Ice Cream Cones

- ◆ 2 cups wheat flour
- ◆ 1 teaspoon baking powder
- ◆ 1/4 teaspoon salt
- ◆ 1/4 cup honey
- ◆ 1/4 cup oil
- ◆ 3/4 cup milk or alternative

Make 12 dummy cones (recipe follows). Combine flour, baking powder and salt in a large bowl. Stir in honey, oil and milk until dough holds together. Divide dough in half. Roll one part into an 11-12 inch circle. Cut into 6 pie shape wedges. Form around dummy cones and seal edge together so there are no openings. Repeat with other half of dough in the same manner. Place cones down on a cookie sheat and bake at 325° for 15 minutes. Turn off oven without removing cones and leave in another 15 to 20 minutes until crisp. Makes 12 cones.

Dummy Cones

- ◆ 8 1/2 x 11 paper

For each cone, fold paper in half. Find the center on the folding edge of paper, this is the end point. Hold the end point with a finger and start rolling paper, making sure the end point is at the bottom and the paper forms into a cylinder shape. Secure outside flap with tape and trim edges straight. Wrap completely with aluminum foil, folding edges into the center of the cone.

"The Lord foresaw the situation of today when motives for money would cause men to conspire to entice others to take noxious substances into their bodies."
President Ezra Taft Benson, May 1983

Creole Doughnuts

- 2 tablespoons oil
- 1 tablespoon honey
- 3/4 cup 100° water
- 1/2 cup milk or alternative
- 1 1/2 teaspoon yeast
- 1 beaten egg
- 3 cups wheat flour
- oil for frying

Combine oil, honey, salt, water, milk and yeast in a large bowl. Let stand 5 minutes to soften yeast. Stir in egg and flour slowly, beating constantly until soft dough forms, which can be dropped from a spoon on greased cookie sheet. Let rise 20 minutes. Heat frying oil in a pan to 365°. Drop dough by tablespoonfuls into oil, a few at a time and fry until browned. Do not crowd. Drain on paper towel. Serve with sauces or toppings. Dough may be frozen and thawed.

Milk-Free Doughnuts

- 1 cup water
- 1/4 cup oil
- 1/2 cup honey
- 3/4 cup (6 oz.) tofu
- 3 cups wheat flour
- 1 tablespoon baking powder
- 1/2 teaspoon salt
- oil for frying

Combine water, oil and honey in large bowl. Beat in tofu, then flour, baking powder and salt. Heat oil to 365° and drop by tablespoonfulls into oil and fry until brown. Drain on paper towels. Serve with sauce or toppings.

Glaze for Cookies, Doughnuts & Cakes

- 1/4 cup lemon or orange juice
- 2 tablespoons honey or maple syrup
- 1 tablespoon butter

Combine all ingredients in a saucepan and boil for 3 minutes.

Oat Cake

- 1 cup water
- 1/2 cup butter
- 1 cup honey or maple syrup
- 2 cups oat flour (process rolled oats in a blender)
- 1/2 cup wheat flour
- 1 teaspoon baking soda
- 1/2 teaspoon salt
- 1 1/2 teaspoon cinnamon
- 2 beaten eggs
- 1/2 cup buttermilk or alternative

Combine water, butter and honey in 3 qt. saucepan. Boil and remove from heat. Mix dry ingredients separately, add this to honey mixture. Add eggs and buttermilk. Spoon into greased 9 x 13 cake pan. Bake at 375° for 30 to 40 minutes. Frost with glaze recipe.

"We should do all we can for ourselves first: dieting, resting, taking simple herbs known to be effective, and apply common sense, especially to minor troubles. Then we could send for the elders...Frequently, this is all that is required, and numerous healings can be affected. In serious cases where the problems are not solved, we turn to our skilled and helpful men who can help us so wonderfully."

President Kimball
Speaks Out on Administration to the Sick
New Era, October 1981, p. 50

Fruit Leather

+ 1 1/2 lb. seasonal fruit
+ 1 tablespoon to 1/4 cup water as needed
+ 1/2 cup honey, optional
+ flavorings such as vanilla, lemon or orange rind, optional

Peel, pit and dice fruit. Purée in blender or food processor, adding water if necessary. Add optional ingredients and process to the consistency of applesauce. Line a cookie sheet or drying screen for each 2 cups purée with heavy plastic wrap, securing corners. Spread purée to 1/8 inch thick. Cover with cheesecloth. Dry in food dehydrator or in the sun on warm days bringing inside at night, or set in your car dash in the sun. May dry in gas oven with pilot light, or electric oven at 140°, opening door periodically to let moisture out. Dry until no wet or sticky spots remain. Remove from cookie sheet, roll up and cut.

Firmer Fruits, such as apple or pears
+ 1 1/2 lb. firm fruit
+ 1/4 cup water

Boil peeled and diced fruit in water 3 to 5 minutes, stirring to prevent scorching. Cool and force through sieve. Add optional ingredients and proceed as directed.

Citrus Fruits
+ 1 lb. citrus fruit
+ 1/2 lb. cranberries and/or bananas

Combine fruits and proceed as directed.

Creamy Roll Ups
+ peanut butter, cream cheese, or fruit butter
+ chopped nuts, optional

Spread desired filling on dried fruit leather, sprinkle with nuts, roll and cut.

Halloween Roll Ups
+ 1 1/2 lb. pureed pumpkin

Use as your fruit and proceed as directed.

Nut Butter Bars

- ♦ I cup rolled oats
- ♦ I cup hot water
- ♦ I/2 cup honey or maple syrup
- ♦ I/2 cup softened butter
- ♦ I egg
- ♦ I cup wheat flour
- ♦ I/2 teaspoon baking soda
- ♦ 3/4 cup nut butter (peanut, almond, etc.)
- ♦ I teaspoon vanilla

Soak oats in water. Cream the butter, honey and egg together, then add the oats, flour, soda, nut butter and vanilla. Spread in greased 9 x 13 pan. Bake at 350° for 10 to 15 minutes. Cool and cut. Makes 36 bars.

Devil's Food Cake

- ♦ 2/3 cups honey
- ♦ I/4 cup softened butter
- ♦ I beaten egg
- ♦ I/2 cup buttermilk or alternative
- ♦ I teaspoon vanilla
- ♦ I cup wheat flour
- ♦ 2 tablespoons nutritional yeast
- ♦ I/2 teaspoon salt
- ♦ I teaspoon baking soda
- ♦ 2 tablespoons carob or cocoa powder
- ♦ I/2 cup hot water

Cream honey and butter, add egg, buttermilk and vanilla. Sift dry ingredients together and add to honey mixture alternately with water. Pour into a greased and floured 9 x 9 cake pan. Bake at 350° for 40 minutes. Serves 9.

Vanilla Yogurt Topping

- ♦ 1 egg yolk
- ♦ 1 cup plain yogurt
- ♦ 1/2 teaspoon vanilla
- ♦ 1 egg white
- ♦ 3 tablespoons honey

Beat yolk and then add the yogurt and vanilla. Beat egg white until stiff, then beat in honey, fold into yogurt mixture.

Honey Glaze

- ♦ 3/4 cup honey
- ♦ 2-4 egg whites
- ♦ dash of cream of tartar
- ♦ salt to taste
- ♦ 1 teaspoon vanilla, almond, anise or lemon extract or food grade essential oil

Combine ingredients and beat on high until fluffy.

Brownies

- ♦ 1 cup carob or cocoa powder
- ♦ 1 cup oil
- ♦ 2/3 cups honey or maple syrup
- ♦ 4 eggs
- ♦ 1 cup ground peanuts (in chopper or blender)
- ♦ 5 tablespoons rye flour
- ♦ 1 cup chopped walnuts, optional
- ♦ 2 teaspoons vanilla

Combine cocoa powder, oil and honey. Separately, beat the eggs until light, then add cocoa mixture. Stir in ground peanuts, rye, nuts and vanilla. Spread batter in greased 8 inch square pan. Bake at 325° for 30 minutes. Yields 16 squares.

Culva

Mediterranean Dessert
- ◆ 2 pt. cooked wheat
- ◆ 1 tablespoon cinnamon
- ◆ 1/2 cup ground walnuts
- ◆ 3 tablespoons honey

Blend together and enjoy.

Better Than Rice Krispie Treats

By far my kids' favorite and so easy!
- ◆ 1/2 cup honey
- ◆ 1/2 cup almond butter
- ◆ 1/4 cup peanut butter
- ◆ 2 teaspoons vanilla
- ◆ 1/2 cup grain sweetened chocolate chips
- ◆ 3 1/2 cup whole grain cereal like crispy brown rice, puffed wheat, etc.

Combine honey and nut butters in a large pan and heat on low until melted. Add vanilla. Separately combine cereal and chocolate chips. Pour cereal mixture into honey mixture and stir well to coat. Pack tightly into a 7 x 11 pan, cool and cut into squares. You may have to adjust cereal measurement to get the bar consistency just right.

Recipe Favorites

Milk, Eggs, Red Snapper, Shad, Turkey, Apple, Apricot, Avocado, Cherry, Grapefruit, Lemon, Mango, Nectarine, Orange, Peach, Rhubarb, Strawberry, Artichoke, Arugula, Asparagus, Beet, Bok Choy, Broccoli, Carrots, Chicories, Collard Greens, Corn, Dandelion, Endive, Fennel, Kale, Lettuce, Greens, Mushroom, Mustard Greens, Okra, Onion, Parsnip, Peas, Potatoes, Radish, Scallion, Sorrel, Spinach, Swiss Chard, Turnip

Spring

Spring Breakfasts

Cheese Bread

Scottish-Irish Breakfast.
- 2 tablespoons water
- 2 cups shredded Longhorn cheese (or favorite cheese)
- 1 beaten egg
- 6 slices whole grain bread or toast
- salt and pepper to taste

Boil water over low heat in a skillet, add cheese, stirring until melted. Stir in egg and cook until the white sets. Spoon onto bread and season.

Nutty Fruity French Toast

- 1/2 cup peanut butter
- 1/2 cup chopped raisins
- 2 tablespoons fruit preserves
- 12 slices of whole grain bread
- 2 eggs
- 1/2 cup milk
- 2 tablespoons butter
- cinnamon to taste

Combine peanut butter, raisins, preserves and cinnamon. Spread mixture on 6 slices of bread. Top each with remaining bread to make a sandwhich. Beat eggs and milk in a wide, shallow bowl. Dip sandwiches in this mixture, drain excess and brown each side in melted butter on a heated skillet. Serves 6.

Fruit Cheese Toast

+ 1/4 cup butter
+ 3 eggs
+ 3 tablespoons milk
+ 8 slices whole grain, stale works well
+ 3 oz. softened cream cheese
+ 1 chopped apple, pear or banana
+ 1/2 teaspoon lemon juice
+ 1/4 cup raisins
+ honey, optional

Heat oven to 450°. Melt butter in a jelly roll pan in the oven and spread evenly. Beat 2 eggs and one egg white (reserve yolk) with milk in bowl. Dip bread in egg mix, coating both sides, place in buttered pan and bake 5 minutes. Mix cream cheese and remaining egg yolk. Separately combine fruit with lemon juice and raisins. Remove bread from oven, turn and spread each slice with cream cheese mixture. Top with fruit mixture. Bake 5 minutes longer, then drizzle with honey. Serves 8.

Rhubarb Muffins

+ 3/4 cup honey
+ 1/4 teaspoon salt
+ 3 tablespoons butter or oil
+ 2 beaten eggs
+ 3/4 cup yogurt or buttermilk
+ 1 teaspoon vanilla
+ 2 cups wheat flour
+ 1 teaspoon baking soda
+ 3 cups chopped rhubarb

Mix honey, salt and butter in a large bowl. Add eggs, yogurt and vanilla and beat well. Add flour, wheat germ and baking soda, stirring until just moistened. Fold in rhubarb. Fill greased muffin cups 2/3 full. Bake at 375° for 20 to 25 minutes. Makes 12 muffins.

Apricot Quinoa-Millet Cereal

- 1 1/2 cup water
- 1 cup apricot jam
- 1 cup chopped apricots
- 1 teaspoon cinnamon
- 1/4 teaspoon mace
- 1/2 cup uncooked quinoa
- 1/2 cup uncooked millet
- 1/4 cup cottage cheese, optional
- 2 tablespoons maple syrup

Boil water, jam, apricots, cinnamon and mace. Add quinoa and millet, simmer covered 15-20 minutes. Press cottage cheese through cheesecloth and add curds and maple syrup to cereal.

Easy Strawberry Jam

- 2 cups sliced strawberries
- 2 tablespoons maple syrup

Combine strawberries and syrup in large frying pan over medium high heat, mashing berries as they cook. Once juicy, simmer until thickened, stirring frequently about 7 minutes. Cool and store covered in the refrigerator up to 2 weeks. Makes 2 to 4 jars, depending on size.

Spring Lunches

Linguine and Spinach

- 2 teaspoons oil
- 2 minced garlic cloves
- 2 cups fresh spinach
- 4 chopped tomatoes
- 4 cups cooked linguine, 1/2 uncooked (brown rice pasta preferred)
- 2 tablespoons Parmesan cheese

Heat oil in skillet and sauté garlic, spinach and tomatoes 3 minutes. Combine with cooked pasta and Parmesan. Serves 4 to 6.

Artichoke Gondolas

- ◆ 4 medium cooked artichokes
- ◆ 3/4 cup sundried tomatoes
- ◆ I small eggplant peeled and diced
- ◆ 2 cups stock
- ◆ 1/4 cup chopped onion
- ◆ I teaspoon basil
- ◆ I teaspoon oregano
- ◆ I-2 minced garlic cloves
- ◆ 1/4 teaspoon salt
- ◆ 1/4 tsp.pepper

Halve the artichokes lengthwise. remove and discard center petals and fuzzy centers. Remove outer leaves and reserve. Trim out hearts and chop finely; set aside. Pour boiling water over tomatoes and let stand 3 minutes to rehydrate; drain and set aside. Simmer eggplant in stock for 10 minutes and drain. In a blender or food processor combine tomatoes, eggplant, onion, herbs, garlic, salt and pepper until smooth. Stir in chopped artichoke hearts. Makes 2 cups. To serve: Arrange reserved artichoke leaves on a platter and spoon I teaspoon of mixture onto the wide end of the leaf. Makes 4 servings.

British Potato Salad

- ◆ 1/2 lb. new potatoes, sliced
- ◆ 1/2 lb. green beans
- ◆ I tablespoon basil
- ◆ I minced shallot
- ◆ I tablespoon cider vinegar
- ◆ I teaspoon oil
- ◆ 3 tablespoons buttermilk
- ◆ salt and pepper to taste

Boil potatoes for 4 minutes, add green beans and simmer 4 minutes. Combine remaining ingredients in a blender or processor. Toss potatoes and beans with processed mixture. Serves 4.

Bulgar Dish

- ◆ 1/2 cup uncooked bulgar wheat
- ◆ 1/2 cup hot stock
- ◆ juice of 1 lemon
- ◆ 1 cup peas
- ◆ 1/2 cup chopped parsely leaves
- ◆ 1 julienned carrot
- ◆ 1 tablespoon olive oil
- ◆ salt to taste

Combine bulgar, stock and lemon juice and soak 20 minutes. Meanwhile simmer peas about 3 minutes, drain and toss with bulgar along with remaining ingredients. Serves 2.

Artichoke and Asparagus Salad

(with stawberry dressing)
- ◆ lettuce leaves
- ◆ 6 sm. steamed artichokes
- ◆ 1 lb. cooked and chilled asparagus
- ◆ 3/4 cup shredded red cabbage

On 6 salad plates, arrange lettuce leaves. Halve the artichokes lengthwise, remove and discard petals and fuzzy centers. Trim out hearts and slice thinly. Arrange artichoke slices on the lettuce with asparagus spears and cabbage. Add artichoke leaves for garnish. Spoon on dressing (recipe follows). Serves 6.

Strawberry Dressing

- ◆ 1/2 cup buttermilk
- ◆ 1 cup sliced fresh strawberries
- ◆ 2 teaspoons honey
- ◆ 1/4 teaspoon allspice

Combine in a blender all ingredients and pulverize until smooth. Yields 1 1/4 cups.

Kashi Salad

- 1 3/4 cup water
- 3/4 tsp. salt
- 1 cup less 2 tablespoons uncooked kashi
- 1 cup chopped red and green bell peppers
- 3 tablespoons chipped scallions
- 2 tablespoons fresh chopped parsley
- 2 tablespoons oil
- 1 tablespoon red wine vinegar, optional

Boil water in 2 qt. saucepan and stir in kashi. Simmer covered 1 hour. Meanwhile combine the peppers, scallions and parsely. Add oil and vinegar. Toss with kashi. Serves 6.

Curried Fry Bites

- 1 1/4 cup cooked garbanzo beans
- 1 egg
- 1/2 cup cooked amaranth, millet or quinoa
- 1 tablespoon curry
- 2 teaspoons chopped cilantro
- 1 minced garlic clove
- 1/2 teaspoon salt
- 1/4 teaspoon red pepper
- 1/2 cup any grain flour
- oil for frying

Purée beans in a blender or processor and add egg, purée. Add grain, curry, cilantro, garlic, salt and pepper and process. Add flour and process again. Heat oil in skillet or deep fryer 2-inches deep until it begins to "pop." Pour batter by the spoonful into the oil and brown both sides. It's important that the oil not be too hot, otherwise the center will not cook. Drain on paper towels. Serve with dipping sauce, preferably a yogurt based one. Yields 30 bites.

Peas and Cheese

- 2 chopped hard-boiled eggs
- 1 cup cubed cheddar cheese
- 2 tablespoons chopped pickle
- 1 tablespoon chopped onion
- 2 cups cooked peas
- 1 cup chopped celery
- 1/4 cup yogurt
- 1/4 cup mayonnaise

Combine all ingredients and chill. Serves 5.

Creamy Beet Salad

- 6 fresh beets
- 1 thinly sliced red onion
- 1 cup thinly sliced cucumber
- 5 T. yogurt or sour cream
- 2 tablespoons mayonnaise
- 1 tablespoon red wine vinegar
- 1/2 teaspoon mustard
- 4 tablespoons minced fresh dill
- salt and pepper to taste

Scrub, top and tail beets, boil in salted water for 45 minutes. Drain and cover with cold watr to cool. Slice beets thinly and transfer to salad bowl, adding the onion and cucumber. Separately combine the remaining ingredients and toss with the vegetables, refrigerate 2 hours. Serves 4 to 6.

Spinach Pie

- 2 lb. fresh, steamed and chopped spinach
- 2 beaten eggs
- 3/4 cup wheat germ
- 1/2 cup cubed Swiss or white cheddar cheese
- 1 tablespoon Worcestshire sauce
- salt and pepper to taste
- 1 minced garlic clove
- 1 unbaked homemade pie shell or rice crust (see Year Round Basics)

Combine ingredients, except pie shell. Spoon mixture into pie shell in a pie plate. Bake at 400° for 25 minutes. Serves 6.

Cornsicles

- ◆ 6 ears of corn, with husks
- ◆ I teaspoon salt
- ◆ I/4 teaspoon pepper
- ◆ I tablespoon chopped fresh oregano
- ◆ I2 medium shrimp, peeled, deveined and diced
- ◆ 24 popsicle sticks

Trim corn, removing husks and silk, save and wash the larger husks. Cut the corn off the cob, scraping out as much milk as possible. Grind the kernels in a food processor, add remaining ingredients. Drop mixture by the tablespoonful onto the center of a clean husk. Fold the left side of the husk into the center, then right, then fold the bottom end upward. Push a popsicle stick 2-3 inches into the open end and pinch the husk around the stick with your fingers. Tear a thin strand from a dry husk and tie it around the cornsicle. Place the rolls, sticks in the air and very close together, in a glass baking dish or loaf pan. Bake at 325° for 30 minutes until corn mixture is firm and solid. To eat, peel the husk and eat it hot from the stick as you would a popsicle. Yields 24/ serves 3.

Corn Fritters

- ◆ 4-5 ears of corn (2 cups)
- ◆ 3 beaten eggs
- ◆ 2 tablespoons cream
- ◆ 2 tablespoons snipped chives or minced green onions
- ◆ I teaspoon salt
- ◆ 3-4 tablespoons flour
- ◆ 3-4 tablespoons oil

Scrape kernels off the ears, you should have 2 cups. Combine everything but the flour and oil in a bowl. Stir in enough flour to form a thick batter. Heat 2 tablespoons of oil and drop batter by the spoonfuls, heating 1-2 minutes per side. Yields 10-12 fritters.

Polenta

- 1 cup fine grind yellow cornmeal or grits
- 3 cups milk
- 1/4 cup Parmesan, optional
- 1 tablespoon butter
- fresh herbs as desired, optional

In 3 qt. saucepan, boil milk and butter. Turn off heat and whisk in cornmeal and stir until thickened 4 minutes. Add Parmesan and herbs. Cover and let sit until set. Unmold it on a cutting board and cut 3/4 inch slices. Saute, broil or bake slices and add toppings or add to recipe.

Mediterranean Topping
- 1 cup thinly sliced onions
- 1 tablespoon oil
- 2 cups broccoli florets
- 1/2 cup sliced mushroom
- 1 cup sliced yellow squash
- 1 cup crushed tomatoes
- 1 1/2 tablespoons coriander
- 1 1/2 teaspoon fresh savory
- 1 teaspoon fresh thyme
- 1/4 teaspoon hot pepper sauce, optional

Heat oil and sauté onions 5 minutes. Add broccoli, mushrooms and squash, sauté an additional 5 minutes. Add remaining ingredients and simmer covered 20 minutes. Serve over polenta.

Primavera Sauce
- 1 cup julienned carrots
- 1 cup julienned zucchini
- 1/2 cup julienned scallions
- 3 tablespoons flour
- 3 tablespoons oil
- 1 1/2 cup milk
- 3 tsp. fresh dill
- 3 tablespoons Parmesan

Steam carrots, zucchini and scallions 4 minutes. Combine milk, flour and oil, boil and simmer constantly until thickened, then add dill. Add to vegetables or serve over polenta.

Asparagus Topping

- 2 cups sliced asparagus
- 1 cup sliced mushrooms
- 1/2 cup minced shallot
- 2 tablespoons stock
- 1 teaspoon oil
- 2 teaspoons snipped chives
- 1 teaspoon fresh tarragon
- 1/2 cup shredded Colby cheese

Steam asparagus 5 minutes. Heat oil in large frying pan and sauté mushrooms, shallots and stock until tender. Add remaining chives, tarragon and asparagus and heat through. Sprinkle with cheese and serve over polenta.

Indian Pudding

- 4 cups milk
- 1 cup maple syrup
- 1/4 cup butter
- 2/3 cups cornmeal
- 1/2 teaspoon ground ginger
- 1/4 teaspoon nutmeg
- 1 1/2 cup raisins

Combine 3 cups milk and syrup in a saucepan over medium heat, boil and add butter. In separate bowl, combine the cornmeal, ginger and nutmeg. Gradually stir the cornmeal mixture into the hot milk. Reduce heat and cook until thickened, 10 minutes. Fold in raisins. Spoon mixture into a buttered 2 qt. casserole dish. Pour remaining milk over pudding; do not stir. Bake at 300° for 2 1/2 hours. Serves 6.

Spring Dinners

Artichoke Quiche

- ◆ 3 slices of wheat bread
- ◆ 1 tablespoon oil
- ◆ 1 teaspoon thyme
- ◆ 1/2 teaspoon paprika
- ◆ 2 cups cottage cheese
- ◆ 3 whisked eggs
- ◆ 2 tablespoons Parmesan cheese
- ◆ 12 oz. cooked artichoke hearts

Pulverise bread in blender or processor. Combine crumbs, oil, thyme and paprika and press into the bottom and sides of a 9 inch pie plate. Bake at 400° for 7 minutes. In a blender or processor, combine cottage cheese, eggs and Parmesan. Separately, pat the artichokes dry and cut into bite size pieces. Add cheese mixture and pour into pie shell. Bake at 350° for 30 minutes.

Penne with Garlic Asparagus

- ◆ 2 teaspoons oil
- ◆ 4 thinly sliced garlic cloves
- ◆ 1/2 lb. sliced asparagus
- ◆ 2/3 cups stock
- ◆ 2 cups cooked whole grain (preferably brown rice) penne pasta
- ◆ 1/4 cup Parmesan

Heat oil and sauté garlic 1 minute. Add stock and asparagus, cover, increase heat to high and let mixture bubble 3 to 4 minutes. Toss with pasta and sprinkle with Parmesan. Serves 4.

Salmon with Chile and Lime

- 12 oz. salmon fillet
- 2 cored and thinly sliced jalapenos
- 2 minced garlic cloves
- juice of 1 lime
- salt to taste
- 1 sliced lemon

Set the fillet skin side down on a large piece of foil. Sprinkle on jalapenos, garlic, lime and salt and then cover with the lemon slices. Seal the foil by folding edges together, then set on a cookie sheet. Bake at 350° for 15 to 20 minutes. Serves 2.

Salmon with Herb Paste

- 2 garlic cloves
- 1 tablespoon minced tarragon
- 1 tablespoon minced parsley
- 1 tablespoon minced thyme
- 1/4 cup lemon juice
- 12 oz. salmon fillet

In a blender or processor combine everything except salmon and process until smooth. Spread the paste on the salmon and grill or broil for about 4 minutes each side. Serves 2.

"Tea as it was consumed in the days of the early Saints, as it is today, was an infusion of the leaves, buds and internodes of the tea plant (Camellia sinensis). Teas derived from this plant [are] black tea, green tea, oolong tea, congou tea, pekoe tea, orange pekoe tea and souchong tea."

Kim Siever / HotPepper.ca

Nasigoreng

Excellent and Easy Malaysian Dish
- ◆ 2 cups cooked rice or grain
- ◆ 4 tablespoons oil, preferably nut oil
- ◆ 2 minced onions
- ◆ 1 minced garlic clove
- ◆ 1 finely shredded red chili
- ◆ 2 skinned, seeded and chopped tomatoes
- ◆ 2 cups cooked and diced chicken (seasonally optional)
- ◆ 6 oz. cooked and diced preferred seafood
- ◆ 2 tablespoons fresh coriander or 2 teaspoons powdered
- ◆ salt and pepper to taste

Heat oil in a large skillet and sauté onion and garlic 2 minutes. Add chili and cook 2 minutes longer. Add tomatoes, chicken and seafood and cook an additional 2 minutes. Add the grain or rice and sauté until golden. Add seasonings and mound on a platter in the oven to keep warm until it's ready for the omelet (below). Serves 4.

Omelet
- ◆ 1 tablespoon oil, preferably nut
- ◆ 3 minced scallions
- ◆ 2 tablespoons soy sauce
- ◆ 4 beaten eggs
- ◆ salt, pepper, paprika to taste

Heat oil in a large skillet and sauté scallions 2 minutes. Season with salt, pepper and soy sauce. Add eggs and cook over low heat until seat. Carefully remove the omelet onto a chopping board and loosely roll. Shred and arrange the shreds over the grain dish and sprinkle with paprika.

65

Millet Salad

♦ 2 cups cooked millet
♦ I cup mung bean sprouts
♦ 1/2 cup (about 16) chopped snow peas
♦ 1/2 cup chopped water chestnuts
♦ 1/4 cup minced green onions
♦ 2 tablespoons oil
♦ I 1/2 tablespoons soy sauce
♦ I tablespoon smooth peanut butter
♦ I tablespoon rice or white vinegar
♦ 1/2 teaspoon sesame or chili oil
♦ I minced garlic clove.

Toss millet, sprouts, peas, water chestnuts and scallion in a large bowl. Separately, combine oil, soy sauce, peanut butter, vinegar, sesame or chili oil and garlic. Toss with millet mixture. Serves 4.

Spinach Mushroom Crepes

♦ I cup minced onion
♦ I 1/2 lb. chopped mushroom
♦ I lb. chopped fresh spinach
♦ 2 tablespoons butter
♦ 30 crepes (Swedish Pancakes) can be made days in advance
♦ I 1/2 lb. shredded Monterey Jack or fresh mozzarella cheese

Heat butter and sauté onion, mushroom and spinach for 10 minutes. Sprinkle thin layer of cheese on one side of the pancake and spoon 1 to 2 tablespoons of the spinach mixture down the center and roll. Place seam side down on oiled baking dish. Repeat with remaining pancakes and sprinkle on remaining cheese. Bake at 350° for 15 minutes. Serves 10.

Eggs à la Golden Rod

Jones Family Favorite

- 2 tablespoons butter
- 2 tablespoons flour
- 1 cup milk or alternative
- salt to taste
- 5 hard-boiled eggs
- loaf of whole grain bread

Whisk flour into milk, add butter and salt and heat until boiled. Reduce heat and simmer until thickened, 2 minutes. It boils quickly so do not walk away from the stove. The mixture will continue to thicken as it cools. This is the white sauce. Spread large spoonful of white sauce over a bread slice and top with egg slices, salt, pepper and paprika if desired. Repeat with remaining sauce and bread. Serves 2 to 4.

Black Bean and Spinach Soup

- 2/3 cups dry black beans
- 3 tablespoons minced onion
- 1 teaspoon garlic
- 1 teaspoon peeled and shredded ginger
- 1 teaspoon orange zest
- 6 cups water
- 5 oz. fresh spinach leaves
- 2 teaspoons oil
- dash of pepper
- 4 tablespoons plain yogurt or sour cream
- 1 tablespoon minced cilantro

Boil beans, onion, garlic, orange zest and water 1 hour. Sauté spinach in oil until wilted but still bright green. Add pepper and cool, mince and set aside. Purée 1/3 of beans in a blender or processor and transfer back to the pot. Stir in spinach and heat. Serves 4 to 6.

Swiss Chard Pie

- 1 chopped onion
- 1 minced garlic clove
- 2 tablespoons oil
- 1 bunch Swiss chard, trimmed and chopped
- 6 beaten eggs
- 1 cup shredded cheddar cheese
- 1 teaspoon salt
- 2 homemade pie crusts

Brown onion and garlic in oil, add chard and cook until wilted. Add eggs, cheese and salt, then pour into a pie shell and bake at 400° for 30 to 40 minutes until toothpick comes out clean. Serves 6.

Polenta Torte

Excellent and easy dish. Impressive looking.

- 20 oz. combination steamed spinach and kale
- 2 tablespoons oil
- 1 chopped onion
- 2 minced garlic cloves
- 1/4 lb. medium chopped ham, optional
- 1/4 teaspoon pepper
- 5 cups water
- 1 1/2 cup yellow cornmeal or grits
- 1/2 teaspoon salt
- 3/4 cup grated Romano or Parmesan cheese
- 1 1/2 cup shredded fontina or mozzarella cheese

Squeeze the greens dry. Sauté onion and garlic in oil 5 minutes. Add the greens, ham and pepper and sauté 4 minutes. Butter or grease a 2 1/2 qt. souffle dish, or line an 8 inch springform pan with foil, then butter bottom and sides. Boil 4 cups water in large saucepan. Combine 1 cup of water, cornmeal and salt. Gradually stir this into the boiling water, simmer 10 minutes, stirring constantly. Spread 1/3 of this polenta mixture into the prepared dish. Cover with half the greens, half the Romano and a third of the fontina. Repeat layering one more time. Spread remaining polenta and sprinkle with fontina. Bake at 400° for 30 minutes. Let stand 10 minutes and remove from springform, if using. Serves 8.

Ovenight Onion Soup

- 4 large onions, thinly sliced
- 8 cups stock
- 1 bay leaf, optional
- 8 thick slices of multi grain, or preferred, bread
- 1 cup shredded Swiss or Parmesan cheese

Combine onions, stock and bay leaf in a slow cooker (crock pot). Cook on low for 24 hours. Ladle into oven proof bowls. Top each with a slice of bread and cheese. Broil until cheese melts. Serves 8.

Spaghetti Squash

- 2 lb. spaghetti squash
- 1 cup shredded cheddar cheese
- 1 1/2 cup grated zucchini
- 2 cups sauced tomatoes
- 1 teaspoon oregano
- 1 minced garlic clove
- salt and pepper to taste
- 1/2 cup Parmesan cheese

Halve the squash lengthwise and scoop out seeds. Place cut side down in 2 inches of simmering water. Cook in covered saucepan for 15 minutes. Holding the hot squash with a towel or potholder, run the tines of a fork across the pulp to make the "spaghetti." Mix the strands with the cheese, zucchini, tomato sauce, oregano, garlic, salt and pepper. Spoon back into the shells and sprinkle with Parmesan. Bake at 350° for 20 minutes on a cookie sheet. Serves 4.

"At no time has cocoa or chocolate been included in the prohibitions of the Word of Wisdom, and at no time has the Church said that cocoa is as harmful as coffee. Those who make these claims do so on their own responsibility, and obviously without knowing the facts of the matter."

Elder Mark E. Peterson
Patterns for Living (Bookcraft, 1962), pp. 235-37

Barley, Bean & Corn Burritos

My kids actually liked this!

- 1 1/2 cup cooked black beans
- 1 cup diced tomatoes
- 1/4 cup diced green chiles, optional
- 1 cup uncooked barley
- 2 cups stock
- 3/4 cup white corn
- 1/4 cup minced onion
- 1 tablespoon lime juice
- 1 teaspoon cumin
- 1 teaspoon chili powder
- 1/2 teaspoon cayenne pepper

- 1 minced garlic clove
- 1/4 cup chopped cilantro
- 16 flour tortillas
- 1 cup shredded cheddar cheese
- 2 tablespoons shredded cheddar cheese
- 8 cups thinly sliced curly leaf lettuce, optional
- 2 1/4 cup homemade salsa, optional
- 1 cup sour cream, optional.

Combine beans, tomatoes, chiles, barley, stock, corn, onion, lime juice, cumin, chili powder, cayenne pepper and garlic. Place in a crock pot on low 4-5 hours, add cilantro. Warm tortillas, place cheese and mixture down the center and roll. Place 1 cup of lettuce on each plate and top with 2 burritos. Garnish with sour cream, salsa and cheese.

"I preached to a large congregation at the stand, on the science and practice of medicine, desiring to persuade the saints to trust in God when sick, and not in the arm of flesh, and live by faith and not by medicine, or poison; and when they were sick, and had called for the Elders to pray for them, and they were not healed, to use herbs and mild food."

History of the Church 4:414

Polenta
& Black Bean Casserole

One of my favorites.
- 3/4 cup chopped fresh cilantro
- 1 cup diced green chiles
- 1/4 cup salsa verde (tomatillos salsa)
- 3 minced garlic cloves
- 1 1/2 teaspoon ground cumin
- 2 cups (10 oz.) polenta, cut into slices
- 1/2 cup whipping cream
- 1 1/2 cup cooked black beans
- 1 1/2 cup cooked hominy or white kidney beans
- 3 cups shredded monterey jack cheese

Combine 1/2 cup cilantro, chiles, salsa verde, garlic, cumin in a medium bowl. Arrange polenta slices on the bottom of a greased 11 x 7 baking dish. Drizzle 1/2 cup cream over it and top with half of beans, hominy and chile mixture. Sprinkle with 1 1/2 cup cheese and repeat layering. Cover with foil and bake 20 minutes at 450°. Uncover and bake until top is browned, about 15 minutes. Let stand 5 minutes and sprinkle with remaining cilantro.

Un-Chicken
Fried Dinner Casserole

Tastes exactly like chicken. Thanks Lisa & Cherida.
- 1 3/4 cup rolled oats
- 1 cup minced onions
- 4 eggs
- 3 tsp. multi herb seasoning
- 1 teaspoon sage
- 5 tablespoons oil
- 3 cups homemade cream of mushroom soup
- 2-3 cups cooked rice or grain

Combine oats, onion and seasonings and form into patties. Heat oil and brown patties on both sides. It will look dry and ugly. Place atop the rice or grain in a casserole dish and pour the soup over for gravy. Heat 350° for 30 minutes.

Spring Sides and Breads

Rhubarb Bread

- ◆ 2 1/2 cups wheat flour
- ◆ 1 teaspoon baking soda
- ◆ 1 teaspoon salt
- ◆ 2/3 cups oil
- ◆ 1 1/2 cup honey
- ◆ 1 egg
- ◆ 1 teaspoon vanilla
- ◆ 1 cup buttermilk
- ◆ 2 cups chopped rhubarb
- ◆ 1/2 cup chopped walnuts, optional

Mix flour, soda and salt. Separately, combine oil, honey, egg, vanilla and buttermilk. Add dry ingredients and stir in rhubarb and walnuts. Pour into 2 loaf pans and bake at 350° for 1 hour. Serves 12.

Popovers

Also Known As Yorkshire Pudding

Simple and crowd pleaser. Jones Family Favorite.

- ◆ 1 1/4 cup milk
- ◆ 1 1/4 cup flour
- ◆ 1/2 teaspoon salt
- ◆ 3 eggs

Whisk milk, flour and salt, but do not overbeat. Add eggs one at a time and blend. Fill greased muffin cups 3/4 full. Bake at 400° for 20 minutes, then reduce to 325° for 15 minutes or until browned. Makes 20 popovers. May also pour batter in a buttered skillet and cook covered on medium heat until set, about 20 minutes. Skillet method will not produce the "popped over" effect.

Green Beans with Dill and Almonds

- 2 cups stock
- 2 sprigs fresh dill weed
- 2 garlic cloves, halved
- 3 lemon slices
- 1 lb. green beans
- 1 tablespoon slivered almonds
- salt to taste

Simmer stock, dill, garlic and lemon. Add beans and simmer covered for 4 minutes. Toast almonds in a separate skillet and add to drained green beans. Great with fish dishes.

Spinach Risotto

- 5 cups stock
- 1 1/2 cup arborio rice
- 1 teaspoon curry
- 1 1/2 cup chopped spinach
- 1/2 cup minced scallions
- 2 tablespoons Parmesan cheese

Bring stock to a boil. Meanwhile heat oil and sauté rice and curry 3 minutes. Add stock and simmer uncovered about 25 minutes until liquid is absorbed. Stir in spinach, scallions and cheese. Serves 4 to 6.

Italian Fried Rice

- 8 artichoke hearts
- 1 cup thinly sliced onions
- 2 minced garlic cloves
- 1 minced shallot
- 3 tablespoons oil
- 2 cups shredded spinach
- 4 cups cold cooked brown rice
- 3 tablespoons Parmesan cheese

Heat 1 tablespoon oil in a skillet and sauté artichoke hearts, onions, garlic and shallots 4 minutes. Add spinach and sauté until wilted. Transfer to a large bowl. Heat 2 tablespoons oil and sauté rice. Add artichoke mixture. Sprinkle with cheese. Serves 6.

Stuffed Peaches

♦ 4 large peaches, preferably white peaches
♦ 2 tablespoons lemon juice
♦ 1/4 cup chopped raisins
♦ 1 tablespoon honey
♦ 1 teaspoon vanilla
♦ 1 teaspoon grated lemon rind
♦ 1/2 teaspoon cinnamon
♦ 3/4 cup plain yogurt

Scald peaches in boiling water 1 minute to loosen skins. Slip off skin, cut peach in half and discard pit. Brush peaches with lemon juice to prevent browning. With a spoon, remove half the pulp from each peach, leaving a sturdy shell. Brush insides with lemon juice and chop removed pulp. Combine raisins, honey, vanilla, lemon rind and cinnamon in a small bowl. Add peach pulp and fold in yogurt to bind stuffing. Divide stuffing among peach halves. Serves 8.

Sprout Ball

For dipping vegetables and crackers.

♦ 1/2 cup wheat sprouts
♦ 1 cup alfalfa sprouts
♦ 1 cup cream cheese
♦ 1/2 cup softened cheddar cheese, optional
♦ 1/2 teaspoon salt
♦ 1 teaspoon minced onion
♦ wheat germ

Mix all ingredients, except wheat germ, and form into a ball. Roll in wheat germ and chill.

Sprout Dip

- 1/2 cup wheat sprouts
- 1/2 cup alfalfa sprouts
- 1/2 cup plain yogurt
- 2 tablespoons chopped chives or parsley

- 1/2 teaspoon salt
- 1/2 cup cream cheese
- 1/4 cup mayonnaise
- 1/2 teaspoon celery seed
- dash of pepper

Mix ingredients and chill.

Cream Cheese or Ricotta Cheese

- 4 cups plain yogurt

Line a large bowl with cheesecloth, or cut the feet off of clean pantyhose at the knee. Spoon in yogurt and tie the corners of the cheese cloth or knot the top of the pantyhose. Hang on a kitchen faucet or tie on a wooden spoon across a pot and let the whey drain from the yogurt 12 hours or overnight. You'll have 1 1/2 to 2 cups of yogurt cheese. Store covered in the refrigerator. This has a sour taste, but works well in recipes.

"When God first made man upon the earth, he was a different being entirely to what he is now; his body was strong, athletic, robust, and healthy; his days were prolonged upon the earth; he lived nearly one thousand years, his mind was vigorous and active, and his intellectual faculties clear and comprehensive, but he has become degenerated...(the Lord) has appointed the word of wisdom as one of the engines to...remove the beastly appetites, the murderous disposition, and the vitiated taste of man; to restore his body to health, and vigour, promote peace between him and the brute creation."

Hyrum Smith, Times and Season,
6-1-1842, pp. 799-800

Cottage Cheese

- ◆ I qt. milk (not boiled, reconstituted, canned or long life milk)
- ◆ active culture yogurt or junket rennet tablet (available at pharmacies), if using pasteurized milk

If using raw, untreated milk, simply stand the container of milk for 1 to 2 days at 75° until set. If using pasteurized milk, add 1 tablespoon yogurt or rennet tablet per quart of milk as a starter. After the milk has set, whether by starter or natural acid formation, heat it slowly, stirring frequently at about 120°. Pour off whey through a cheesecloth. Drain the curds to desired constistency and add a little salt.

Egg Foo Yung

- ◆ 5 eggs
- ◆ 1/2 cup water
- ◆ 1/4 cup chpped onions
- ◆ 1/2 cup mung bean sprouts
- ◆ 1/2 cup sliced mushrooms
- ◆ salt and pepper to taste
- ◆ 1-2 teaspoons soy sauce
- ◆ 1 tablespoon oil

Beat eggs and water for 5 minutes. Add onions, sprouts, mushrooms, salt, pepper and soy sauce. Heat oil in a skillet, pour batter and turn heat to low. Cook 3 minutes each side. Serves 4.

Spring Desserts

Strawberry Pie

- 2 cups chopped strawberries
- 3/4 cup water
- 3/4 cup honey
- salt to taste
- 2 tablespoons flour
- 1 1/2 tablespoons water
- 3 oz. cream chese
- 1 tablespoon honey
- 2 teaspoons lemon juice
- 1/2 teaspoon vanilla
- 1 baked homemade oil pie crust
- 2 cups whole strawberries

Combine the chopped strawberries, 3/4 cup water, 3/4 cup honey and salt in a saucepan and boil 2 minutes, then strain. Blend flour and 1 1/2 teaspoon water in a cup. Stir into strained mixture in saucepan and cook until thickened, stirring constantly, then cool. Separately, combine the cream cheese, 1 tablespoon honey, lemon juice, vanilla and the salt to taste. Spoon into pie shell. Arrange the whole strawberries over this, then top with thickened glaze. Garnish with whipped cream. Serves 8.

Peach Souffle

- 1 1/2 cup diced peaches
- 3 tablespoons honey
- 1 tablespoon lemon juice
- 1/2 teaspoon nutmeg
- 5 egg whites
- 1/8 teaspoon cinnamon

Purée peaches, then combine it with honey in a saucepan and simmer 20 minutes. Add lemon juice and nutmeg, then cool. Beat egg whites in a large bowl until stiff peaks form. Fold 1/3 of whites in peach mixture. Then fold peach mixture into remaining whites. Spoon mixture into an ungreased souffle dish and sprinkle with cinnamon. Place dish in a pan of hot water. Bake at 300° for 1 hour. Do not open oven door or souffle will fall. Serve immediately.

Strawberry Rhubarb Dessert Sauce

- ◆ 1 cup sliced stawberries
- ◆ 3 cups sliced rhubarb
- ◆ 1/2 cup orange juice, with pulp

Combine all ingredients in a saucepan over medium heat, mashing fruit as you go and bring mixture to a boil as the juice is released. Reduce heat to low and simmer, stirring frequently about 15 to 20 minutes. Serve atop fruit freezes, fruit salads, or crepes.

Cheesecake

- ◆ 1 recipe homemade graham cracker crust
- ◆ 4 cups (24 oz.) cream cheese, cottage cheese, or yogurt cheese
- ◆ 3/4 cup (3 to 5) eggs
- ◆ 1/4 cup honey, maple syrup, barley malt, or molasses
- ◆ 1-2 tablespoons grated lemon zest
- ◆ 1/4 cup lemon juice with pulp

Line a 10 inch spring form pan with the crust mixture. Purée remaining ingredients in blender or processor and spoon atop the crust. Bake at 350° for 45 to 60 minutes. Serves 6.

Peanut Butter Satin

Excellent by itself or as a pie filling.

- ◆ 1/2 cup nut butter (peanut, almond, etc)
- ◆ 1/2 cup softened butter
- ◆ 1/4 cup honey
- ◆ 1 teaspoon vanilla
- ◆ 3-4 eggs

Cream the nut butter, butter, honey and vanilla. Add eggs, one at a time, beating in a mixer at high speed for at least 5 minutes each addition. If it doesn't whip as desired, be sure you have beaten the full 5 minutes per egg or chill well, then finish beating.
Sprinkle with chocolate or carob chips. Serves 12, 1/4 cup servings.

Half Moons

- ♦ 4 cups apricots or in season fruit
- ♦ 1/4 cup honey or maple syrup
- ♦ ground allspice to taste
- ♦ 2 homemade oil pie crust dough

Mash fruit and add honey and allspice. Roll out dough on a floured surface and cut eight, 5-inch circles. Place on cookie sheet and spoon the filling onto half the circles. Fold dough over, pressing edges to seal. Prick tops with fork and bake at 400° for 30 minutes. Serves 8.

Cream Cheese Frosting

- ♦ 1 cup (8 oz.) cream cheese
- ♦ 1/2 cup softened butter
- ♦ 4 tablespoons honey or maple syrup
- ♦ 1 teaspoon vanilla
- ♦ 1/2 cup chopped pecans, optional

Beat cheese and butter until fluffy, add in remaining ingredients. Makes 2 cups.

Banana Nut Cream Cheese Frosting

above recipe
- ♦ 1 mashed ripe banana

Follow above directions, adding the banana with the cheese.

Fudge Pie

- ♦ 3/4 cup carob powder
- ♦ 1/2 cup honey
- ♦ 1/2 cup softened butter
- ♦ 3 eggs
- ♦ 1 tablespoon vanilla, optional

Beat all ingredients until smooth. Pour into a greased pie plate and bake at 350° for 20 minutes. Cut into wedges. Serves 8.

Sponge Cake

- ♦ 3/4 cup rice flour
- ♦ 1/4 teaspoon salt
- ♦ 7 eggs, separated
- ♦ 1/4 cup honey or mape syrup
- ♦ 2 tablespoons lemon juice
- ♦ 2 tablespoons grated lemon rind
- ♦ 1/2 teaspoon vanilla

All ingredients need to be at room temperature. Sift flour and salt together, set aside. Beat yolks at medium speed and gradually add honey, beating until dissolved. Add lemon juice, rind and vanilla. Add flour slowly. Beat egg whites on high speed and fold 1/4 of them into yolk mixture. With an under-over motion using a rubber spatula, fold yolk mixture into remaining whites, but do not over mix. Prepare two 9-inch layer cake pans by cutting 2 circles from heavy parchment or brown paper to fit the bottom of each pan. Oil pans lightly and place paper in the bottom. Pour batter into pans and bake on middle rack at 325° for 30 minutes. Remove and cool 10 minutes. Loosen sides with spatula and invert to wire rack, removing paper immediately. Frost as desired. Serves 12.

"There is no question that the health of the body affects the spirit, or the Lord would never have revealed the Word of Wisdom. God has never given any temporal commandments; that which affects our stature affects our soul."

In His Steps, address given by President Ezra Taft Benson of the Council of the Twelve Apostles Fourteen-Stake Fireside Address, Brigham Young University, March 4, 1979

Carob Almond Cake

- 2/3 cups carob or cocoa powder
- 1/2 cup boiling water
- 6 tablespoons honey or maple syrup
- 3/4 cup oil
- 1 teaspoon vanilla
- 6 room temperature eggs, separated
- 3/4 cup ground nuts, almonds recommended
- 1/4 cup flour, rice flour recommended
- 1/4 teaspoon salt

Combine carob and boiling water, then cool. Combine honey, oil and vanilla. Beat yolks until thick, then add the honey mixture. Blend in carob mixture and beat. Combine ground nuts and flour, then add to batter. Beat egg whites and salt until it peaks. With a whisk, use an under-over motion and gently fold batter into beaten egg whites. Pour batter into a greased, then parchment or brown paper lined 8-inch square pan. Bake on middle rack at 325° for 50 minutes. Remove and cool 15 minutes. Loosen cake from pan with spatula, invert to a wire rack and remove paper. Serve plain or frosted. Serves 10 to 12.

Brown Rice Pudding

- 3 eggs
- 3/4 cup honey or maple syrup
- 2 1/2 cups cooked brown rice
- 3 cups milk or alternative
- 1 teaspoon vanilla
- 1/4 teaspoon ground nutmeg or cloves
- 1/2 teaspoon cinnamon
- 1/2 cup raisins
- 1/2 cup shredded coconut, seasonally optional
- 1/2 cup chopped almonds
- 1 cup crushed pineapple, seasonally optional
- 1/2 cup wheat germ

Beat eggs and honey until smooth. Stir in remaining ingredients. Spoon into a greased 2 1/2 qt. casserole dish. Place in a large pan of hot water. Bake at 350° for 45-60 minutes, or until knife comes out clean. Serves 8.

Recipe Favorites

Apple, Apricot, Banana, Blueberry, Cantaloupe, Cherry, Currant, Fig, Grape, Honeydew, Lemon, Mango, Nectarine, Orange, Papaya, Peach, Pear, Plum, Raspberry, Rhubarb, Strawberry, Watermelon, Arugula, Beet, Broccoli, Cabbage, Celery, Cucumber, Eggplant, Endive, Green Bean, Kohlrabi, Lettuce, Mushroom, Okra, Onion, Pea, Peppers, Radicchio, Summer Squash, Swiss Chard, Tomato

Summer

Summer Breakfasts

Cherry Maple Crunch

- ◆ 3 cups pitted sour cherries
- ◆ 1 teaspoon flour
- ◆ 3/4 cup maple syrup
- ◆ 1/2 cup rolled oats
- ◆ 2 tablespoons oil

Grease 9-inch pie plate and add cherries. Separatly, dissolve flour in maple syrup. Pour over cherries. In a small bowl combine oats and oil and sprinkle over cherries. Bake at 350° for 40 minutes.

Pineapple Muffins

- ◆ 2 cups wheat flour
- ◆ 2 teaspoons baking powder
- ◆ salt to taste
- ◆ 1/4 cup softened butter
- ◆ 1/4 cup honey
- ◆ 1 beaten egg
- ◆ 3/4 cup cubed and crushed pineapple, with juice
- ◆ 1 cup chopped pecans or walnuts, optional

Combine flour, baking powder and salt. Cream butter, honey and egg in large bowl. Add dry ingredients, nuts and pineapple. Fill greased muffin cups 2/3 full and bake at 400° for 20 to 25 minutes.

Breakfast Bars

+ 2 1/2 cups granola or rolled oats
+ 3/4 cup wheat flour
+ 1 teaspoon baking powder
+ 1/4 teaspoon salt
+ 1/4 cup honey
+ 1 mashed banana
+ 1/2 cup melted butter
+ 1 egg
+ 1 teaspoon vanilla

Set 1/2 cup of the granola or oats aside. Combine remaining ingredients. Spread into greased 11 x 17-inch pan. Crush reserved cereal and sprinkle on top. Bake at 350° for 25 minutes. Cool and cut.

Tropical Mush

+ 1 cup sprouted wheat
+ 1/2 cup papaya, chopped
+ 1 mango, chopped

Combine in a blender and purée. Serves 1.

Buckwheat Mush

+ 1 cup sprouted buckwheat
+ 1 banana
+ 5 strawberries
+ 1/2 papaya, chopped

Combine all ingredients in a blender and purée. Serves 1 to 2.

Lemonade with a Twist

Great for nausea, as well as a summer cooler.

♦ 3/4 cup honey
♦ 5 thin slices gingerroot
♦ juice of 8 lemons, at room temperature

Combine honey and gingerroot and heat on low in small saucepan, 5 minutes. Discard root and stir in juice. Combine 5 T. of syrup into 1 cup water or complimentary juice to make lemonade. The syrup will keep, jarred or refrigerated, for 1 month. You can also freeze the syrup in ice cube trays and use to cool water.

Lavender Lemonade

♦ 3/4 cup honey
♦ 3-4 drops of food grade lavender essential oil
♦ juice of 8 lemons, at room temperature

Heat honey and lemon juice in a small saucepan 5 minutes. Add lavender and stir 4 tablespoons syrup into 1 cup water or complimentary juice to make lemonade. Refer to above recipe for freezing instructions, if desired.

Fresh Fruit Tea

♦ 2 sliced strawberries
♦ 1 chopped orange segment
♦ 2 sprigs fresh mint
♦ 2 teaspoons herb leaves of your choice
♦ 2 cups just boiled water

Combine all ingredients and steep, covered, about 2 minutes. Strain and sweeten. Makes 2 cups.

Banana Pancakes

- 1 3/4 cup wheat flour
- 1 1/2 teaspoon baking powder
- 3/4 cup cooked barley
- 1/2 cup milk or alternative
- 1/2 cup mashed bananas
- 2 egg whites
- 2 tablespoons maple syrup
- 2 tablespoons oil
- 2 tablespoons preserves or jam
- 2 sliced bananas
- 2 cups orange segments

Sift flour and baking powder, add barley. Separately whisk milk, mashed banana, egg whites and maple syrup. Combine both mixtures but do not over mix. Heat oil in skillet or grill and cook pancakes as usual. When done, add jam to skillet and stir to melt. Add the bananas and oranges and heat for 3 minutes. Serve over pancakes.

Summer Lunches

Rice, Bean and Corn Salad

- 2 cups cooked brown rice
- 2 cups (16 oz.) cooked red kidney beans
- 1 1/2 cup cut corn
- 4 chopped scallions
- 3 tablespoons olive oil
- 3 tablespoons lime juice
- 3 tablespoons cider vinegar
- 1 tablespoon honey
- 2 minced jalapenos, optional
- 1 teaspoon chili powder
- 1/2 teaspoon cumin
- 1/2 teaspoon salt

Combine all ingredients and serve with lime wedges. Serves 4 to 6.

Corn Salad
with Tomato Dressing

- 2 cups cooked brown rice
- I cup cooked corn kernels
- 3/4 cup minced celery
- I minced shallot
- 1/2 cup chopped and peeled tomato
- I tablespoon lemon juice
- I tablespoon balsamic vinegar
- I 1/2 teaspoon basil
- 1/2 teaspoon thyme
- 1/2 teaspoon mustard
- salt and pepper to taste
- lettuce for serving

Combine rice, corn, celery and shallot in medium bowl. In a blender or processor combine tomato, lemon juice, vinegar, thyme, mustard, salt and pepper and process 25 seconds. Toss with corn mixture and serve over lettuce leaves. Serves 4.

Zucchini "Pasta"

- I cup stock
- 2 minced garlic cloves
- I julienned carrot
- 4 large zucchini, sliced into 1/8-inch strips or julienned (that's the pasta!)
- 1/4 cup Parmesan
- 1/4 cup shredded mozzarella
- 1/4 cup milk or alternative
- 1/4 cup minced fresh basil
- linguine or spaghetti, optional

Combine stock and garlic, heat on high 1-2 minutes. Reduce heat to medium and add carrot. Cover and cook 3 minutes. Add zucchini cover and cook 2 minutes. Drain liquid and toss in remaining ingredients. Serves 2.

Zucchini Milk

Use as milk alternative in recipes.
- 4 fresh medium zucchini

Peel zucchini and cut into chunks and liquify them in a blender or processor. This is the milk. Will keep frozen for 6 months. Makes 4 cups.

Peach and Walnut Salad

- 1 endive, separated into petals
- 2 peeled and sliced peaches, preverably white
- 2 minced scallions
- 2 tablespoons toasted and chopped walnuts
- 1 tablespoon olive or walnut oil
- 2 tablespoons lemon juice
- 1 tablespoon balsamic vinegar
- salt and pepper to taste
- watercress for garnish, optional

On a chilled serving plate, arrange endive petals in a spoke pattern. Arrange the peach slices atop the endive. Sprinkle with scallions and walnuts and garnish with the cress. In a small bowl, combine remaining ingredients and drizzle over salad. Serves 2.

Zucchini Corn Soup

- 2 tablespoons butter
- 3/4 cup thinly sliced leek
- 2 cups shredded zucchini
- 1 3/4 cup stock
- 1 cup corn kernels
- 1/2 cup water
- 1/2 cup milk alternative or zucchini milk

Heat butter in 3 qt. saucepan and sauté leek until soft. Add zucchini, broth 1/2 cup corn and water. Boil, then simmer uncovered 20 minutes. Purée half this mixture in a blender or processor. Remove and purée the other half. Return soup to saucepan and add the remaining corn and milk alternative. Heat through. Serves 6.

Curried Millet Salad

- 2 cups cooked millet
- I cup chopped tomato
- 1/2 cup chopped cucumber
- 1/2 cup chopped green bell pepper
- 1/4 cup sliced scallion
- 2 tablespoons oil
- I tablespoon cider vinegar
- I teaspoon curry powder
- 1/4 teaspoon cinnamon
- 1/4 teaspoon coriander
- 1/4 teaspoon paprika
- salt and pepper to taste

Toss millet, tomato, cucumber, green pepper and scallion in a large bowl. Separately combine remaining ingredients and toss with the millet mixture. Serves 6.

Bean Pesto

Serve with pasta, toast or vegetables.

- 2 cups cooked white beans, cannellini, great northern, etc.
- I cup packed fresh basil leaves
- 2 peeled garlic cloves
- 3 tablespoons olive oil
- I teaspoon salt
- 1/4 teaspoon pepper
- dried toast, optional
- fresh vegetable sticks such as fennel, radishes, peppers, cucumbers, optional
- grain or zucchini pasta, optional

Purée beans, basil and garlic in a blender or processor. Add oil, salt and pepper, then refrigerate 2 hours. Arrange bread slices on a cookie sheet and bake at 350° 4-5 minutes, both sides. To serve, transfer to a serving bowl or hollowed out vegetable and serve with optional items. Yields 2 cups.

Moroccan Salad

- 1 cup dry couscous
- 1/2 teaspoon salt
- 2 cups cooked garbanzo beans
- 1 thinly sliced red bell pepper
- 1 large minced carrot
- 2/3 cups minced red onion
- 1/2 cup sliced black olives
- 1 1/2 cup crumbled feta cheese or firm tofu, optional
- romaine lettuce leaves

Boil 1 1/2 cup water and add couscous and salt. Remove from heat immedietely and let stand 5 minutes. May substitute cooked quinoa for couscous. Transfer to a large bowl and add the garbanzo beans, red pepper, carrot, onion and olives. Pour mint dressing (below) and toss. Add feta or tofu and refrigerate 1 hour. Line platter with lettuce leaves, spoon salad over and garnish with mint sprigs. Serves 4-6.

Mint Dressing

- 1/4 cup lemon juice
- 1 peeled garlic clove
- 1 teaspoon mustard
- 1/4 teaspoon salt
- 1/4 teaspoon pepper
- 1/4 tsp honey
- 3/4 cup mint sprigs
- 2/3 cups olive oil

Combine all ingredients except olive oil in a blender or processer and pulse. With motor running, slowly pour oil in and purée until smooth.

"By a proper observation of the Word of Wisdom, man may hope to regain what he has lost by transgression and live to the age of a tree, that as the sun's rays in springtime gladden all nature and awaken life and hope, the Word of Wisdom given of God may remove the thorns and briers from our pathway and strew the same with joy and peace."

Joseph Smith, Joseph Smith as a Prophet,
Scrapbook of Mormon Literature, Vol. I, p 118

Kumquat & Snow Pea Rice Salad

- 1 cup cooked rice or grain
- 4 kumquats
- 1/4 cup snow peas
- 2 tablespoons slivered toasted almonds
- 1/4 cup oil, preferably peanut
- 2 sliced scallions
- 1 tablespoon peeled and minced ginger
- salt and pepper to taste
- 3 tablespoons minced cilantro

Drop kumquats in boiling water for about 30 seconds. Remove to cold water, then drain. Repeat same process with snow peas. Slice the kumquats thinly into rounds, removing seeds. Slice snow peas on the diagonal and set on the same plate as the kumquats. Heat 1 tablespoon oil in a skillet and sauté scallions about 2 minutes. Add ginger and stir 30 seconds longer. Set the scallions aside, near the almonds. Combine remaining oil, salt and pepper and stir into the rice. Combine all ingredients. Serves 4.

"The Lord has told us what is good for us to eat, and to drink, and what is pernicious, but some of our wise philosophers, and some of our elders too, pay no regard to it; for they think it is too little, too foolish for wise men to regard—fools!...Who made the corn, the wheat, the rye, and all the vegetable substances? And who was it that organized man, and constituted him as he is found? Who made his stomach and his digestive organs, and prepared proper nutriment for his system, that the juices of his body might be supplied; and his form be invigorated by that kind of food which the laws of nature, and the laws of God have said would be good for man? And God made his food and provided it for the use of man."

Joseph Smith, Times and Seasons, Vol. III, No 15,
pages 799-801,
Nauvoo, Illinois, June 1, 1842

Coleslaw

- 1 head of shredded cabbage
- 2 chopped apples
- 1/2 cup chopped dates
- 2 tablespoons sunflower seeds
- 1/2 cup chopped celery, optional
- 1/2 cup chopped green pepper, optional
- 1/2 cup crushed pineapple, optional
- 1/2 cup chopped nuts, optional
- 1-2 chopped oranges, optional

Toss ingredients together and mix in dressing (below). Chill before serving. Serves 8.

Coleslaw Dressing

- 1/4 cup honey
- 3 tablespoons cider vinegar
- 2 tablespoons oil
- Combine together and add to coleslaw.

Yogurt-Mayo Dressing, Seasonally Optional

- 2 cups plain yogurt
- 1 cup mayonnaise or cottage cheese
- 2 teaspoons fresh dill
- 1 teaspoon pepper
- 1 teaspoon mustard
- 1 minced garlic clove

Combine ingredients and mix with coleslaw.

Corn and Pea Soup

- ◆ 1 avocado
- ◆ 2 tomatoes
- ◆ 2 cups boiling water
- ◆ 1/2 cup chopped celery stalk
- ◆ 1 corn cob
- ◆ 1 cup cooked peas
- ◆ 2 tablespoons oil
- ◆ 1 garlic clove
- ◆ juice of 1/2 lemon
- ◆ 1 tablespoon fresh dill

Cut avocado in half, pit and peel. Slice up one half. Blend the other half with tomatoes, garlic and oil in a blender or processor to soupy consistency. Add more water if needed. Add cut corn from the cob and remaining ingredients, including sliced avocado, and heat. Serves 2.

No Cream of Mushroom Soup

- ◆ 1 avocado
- ◆ 1 tomato
- ◆ 1 cup boiling water
- ◆ 1 diced red bell pepper
- ◆ 1 cup sliced mushrooms
- ◆ 1 diced onion
- ◆ 1 garlic clove
- ◆ juice of 1/2 grapefruit
- ◆ 1 tablespoon fresh chopped basil

Peel and pit avocado. Combine avocado, grapefruit juice, garlic and water in a blender and purée to creamy consistency. Add remaining ingredients and heat, or freeze. Serves 2.

Fried Green Tomatoes

- 4 green or slightly red tomatoes
- 2 eggs
- 1/2 cup milk alternative
- 1 cup flour
- 1/2 cup cornmeal
- 1/2 cup breadcrumbs
- 2 teaspoons salt
- pepper to taste
- oil

Slice tomatoes 1/2-inch thick. Pour oil 1/2-inch deep in skillet and heat on medium. Whisk eggs and milk together. Scoop flour onto a plate or shallow bowl. Combine cornmeal, breadcrumbs, salt and pepper on another plate. Dip tomatoes into flour to coat, then dip into egg mixture and dredge breadcrumbs to completely coat. Place tomatoes in the heated oil in batches of 4 and 5, but do not crowd. Fry until browned both sides and drain on paper towels.

Banana Peanut Butter "Sandwiches"

- 3 firm, but ripe, bananas
- 1/2 - 3/4 cup peanut butter
- 1/4 cup orange juice
- 1 cup minced peanuts or shredded coconut

Slice peeled banana in two lengthwise. Spread each half with peanut butter and put back together. Brush with orange juice and roll in peanuts or coconut. Cut into 1-inch "coins." Repeat with remaining bananas.

Summer Dinners

Bulgar and Beans

- 1 1/2 cup uncooked bulgar wheat
- 1 tablespoon olive oil
- 1/2 cup chopped green onions
- 1/2 cup chopped green pepper
- 2 cups water
- 2 large chopped tomatoes
- 1 cup cooked red beans
- 1 minced garlic clove
- dash of black pepper
- 1 teaspoon paprika

Heat oil and sauté bulgar until golden. Add remaining ingredients. Boil, then simmer covered for 15 minutes. Serves 4.

Black Bean Burgers

Easy and Excellent
- 1 teaspoon oil
- 1/2 cup minced onion
- 5 minced scallions, optional
- 1 cup corn kernels
- 1/4 cup homemade salsa
- 1/2 cup cooked brown rice
- 1 1/2 cup (16 oz.) cooked black beans
- 1-2 cups wheat breadcrumbs

Heat oil in medium saucepan and sauté onion and scallions 4 minutes. Add corn and salsa and heat through. Scoop corn mixture, rice, beans and 1 cup breadcrumbs in a food processor and mix well. Check texture by trying to form a patty. If it doesn't hold together, add more breadcrumbs. Divide mixture into 8 patties. Grill or broil on a cookie sheet 5 minutes each side. Serve as you would hamburgers.

Tacos

- 1 chopped onion
- 2 chopped celery stalks
- 1 tablespoon oil
- 2 cups chopped mushrooms or zucchini, optional
- 1 cup sauce of crushed tomatoes
- 1/2 teaspoon cumin
- 2 cups cooked kidney or pinto beans
- 1/2 teaspoon salt
- 20 warmed or fried corn tortillas
- 2 chopped tomatoes, optional
- 1 chopped bell pepper, optional
- 2 cups shredded lettuce or sprouts, optional

Heat oil in large skillet and sauté onions, mushrooms or zucchini and celery. Add tomato sauce, cumin, beans and salt and simmer 15 minutes. Sandwich the filling in the tortilla and add toppings. Serves 10.

Wild Rice and Bean Salad

Also known as Confetti Salad.

- 1 1/4 cup white kidney beans (cannellini)
- 1 1/2 cup wild rice
- 1 cup chopped red bell pepper
- 1/4 cup sliced scallion
- 3 tablespoons olive oil
- 1 tablespoon cider vinegar
- 1 tablespoon lemon juice
- 2 teaspoons spicy brown mustard
- 1 minced garlic clove
- salt and pepper to taste

Combine beans, rice, bell pepper and scallion in large bowl. Separately combine the oil, vinegar, lemon juice, mustard, garlic, salt and pepper and toss with the rice mixture. Serves 6.

Quinoa Stew

Mexican Syle

+ 2 tablespoons oil
+ 1/2 cup uncooked quinoa
+ 1/2 cup chopped onion
+ 1 minced garlic clove
+ 1 3/4 cup squishy, overripe peeled tomatoes
+ 1/4 teaspoon cumin
+ 1/4 teaspoon ground red pepper
+ salt and oregano to taste
+ corn chips or shredded monterey jack cheese, optional

Heat oil in a large saucepan and sauté quinoa, onion and garlic until quinoa starts to crackle. Add remaining ingredients, except cheese, boil, then simmer 20 minutes. Let stand 5 minutes and top with optional cheese or homemade corn chips.

Stuffed Zucchini

+ 4 large zucchini
+ 1-2 cups cooked grain or rice
+ 1 chopped onion
+ 2 chopped tomatoes
+ 1 cup cooked black beans
+ 1 cup cooked corn
+ 1 tablespoon oil
+ 1 minced garlic clove
+ salt and pepper to taste
+ Parmesan cheese for topping, optional

Cut zucchini in half lengthwise and scoop out, then chop the scooped flesh. Heat oil and garlic in skillet and sauté the vegetables, beans and spices. Combine the vegetable mixture with the grains and fill the zucchini boats. Sprinkle with cheese. Bake at 350° for 20 minutes. Serves 4.

Wild Rice and Pine Nuts

(Great party dish when doubled or trippled.)

- ◆ I cup uncooked wild rice
- ◆ 4 cups water
- ◆ I bay leaf
- ◆ 2 tablespoons pine nuts (pignolas)
- ◆ I thinly sliced red bell pepper
- ◆ I thinly sliced yellow bell pepper
- ◆ 2 minced scallions
- ◆ 2 minced garlic cloves
- ◆ I tablespoon minced fresh basil, or dried equivalent
- ◆ 3 tsp. fresh minced thyme or dried equivalent
- ◆ 2 tablespoons balsamic vinegar
- ◆ I tablespoon lemon juice
- ◆ 2 teaspoons olive oil
- ◆ 2 tablespoons feta cheese, optional
- ◆ salt, pepper and mustard to taste

Boil rice, water and bay leaf uncovered for 35 minutes. Drain and discard bay leaf. Meanwhile sauté pine nuts in a dry skillet for 2-3 minutes. Transfer rice to a large bowl, add nuts, bell peppers, scallions, garlic, basil and thyme. In a small bowl whisk vinegar, lemon juice, oil, mustard, salt and pepper. Combine with rice mixture and top with feta. Serves 2.

"It is a piece of good counsel which the Lord desires his people to observe, that they may live on the earth until the measure of their creation is full. This is the object the Lord had in view in giving that Word of Wisdom. To those who observe it He will give great wisdom and understanding, increasing their health, giving strength and endurance to the faculties of their bodies and minds until they shall be full of years upon the earth."

Discourses of Brigham Young, p. 184

Ragout

Middle Eastern Style

- 1 eggplant, 1 1/4 lb., cut in 3/4 inch cubes
- 3 tablespoons olive oil
- 2 cups chopped onion
- 1 chopped green bell pepper
- 3 minced garlic cloves
- 1 tablespoon cumin
- 1 1/2 teaspoon cinnamon
- 1 teaspoon ground ginger
- 1 teaspoon ground coriander
- 1/4 teaspoon cayenne
- 1 3/4 lb. chopped and seeded tomatoes
- 2 cups cooked garbanzo beans
- salt and pepper

Toss eggplant with 1 teaspoon salt. Set aside for 20 minutes, then rinse in cold water and pat dry. Heat oil in large skillet and sauté onion 5 minutes. Add bell pepper and garlic and cook for 2 minutes. Add cumin, ginger, coriander and cayenne and stir for 1 minute. Add eggplant, tomatoes and 1 cup water. Boil, then simmer covered 15 minutes. Add beans and simmer 15 minutes longer. Season with salt and pepper. Serve over couscous or grains. Serves 6.

Rice 'n' Peas

Jamaican Dish

- 8 oz. dry kidney beans
- 1 teaspoon salt
- 2/3 cups coconut milk
- 3 minced garlic cloves
- 3 tablespoons chopped fresh thyme, or dried equivalent
- 2 minced jalapeno peppers
- 1/4 teaspoon allspice
- 2 cups uncooked brown rice
- 1 cup sliced scallion
- 3 tablespoons butter
- salt and pepper to taste

Boil 7 cups of water in a soup pot, add beans and salt. Simmer covered 1-1 1/2 hours. Add coconut milk, garlic, thyme, jalapeno and allspice and simmer 5 minutes. Add rice, scallions and butter and simmer covered about 25 minutes. Add additional liquid if dish seems dry. Season with pepper and salt. Serves 6.

Tabbouleh

Also known as Tabouli.

- ◆ 2 cups cooked bulgar wheat, couscous, cracked wheat or quinoa
- ◆ 1 bunch minced parsely
- ◆ 1-2 chopped tomatoes
- ◆ 3 tablespoons minced mint
- ◆ 1 chopped cucumber
- ◆ 1 minced garlic clove
- ◆ 3 thinly sliced scallions
- ◆ 1/2 cup olive oil
- ◆ 1/4 cup lemon juice

Combine ingredients and chill, marinating 1 hour. Serves 4 to 6.

If thou wilt diligently hearken to the voice of the Lord thy God, and wilt do that which is right in his sight, and wilt give ear to his commandments, and keep all his statutes, I will put none of these diseases upon thee, which I have brought upon the Egyptians: for I am the Lord that healeth thee.

Exodus 15:26

Vegetable Terrine

Easy and looks incredible.
- olive oil as needed
- 1 head cabbage, separated and blanched
- 6 portobello mushrooms, roasted
- 6 yellow bell peppers, roasted
- 1 eggplant, roasted
- salt and pepper to taste
- 5 cups hot polenta
- Tomato-Chile Coulisse (below)

Rub the inside of a large metal pate mold with olive oil and line with cabbage leaves, allowing about 2 inches to overhang on all sides. Slice the roasted mushrooms, bell peppers and eggplant and neatly fit them into the mold, layered alternatively, sprinkling lightly with salt and pepper. Repeat 2-3 layers of each vegetable. Pour the polenta into the mold until it almost reaches the top. Fold the overhung cabbage leaves over the polenta to cover completely. Chill until polenta sets. Cover mold with foil and bake at 300° for 25 minutes. Flip the mold over to let it slide out and slice for presentation. Spoon coulisse over it.

Tomato-Chile Coulisse
- 2 tablespoons olive oil
- 1 minced garlic clove
- 1/2 minced chipotle chile
- 3 diced tomatoes
- salt and pepper to taste

Heat oil and sauté garlic. Add tomatoes and cook until completely soft. Purée and season to taste. Strain.

Taco Salad

Jones Family Favorite
- 1/2 cup minced onion
- 1 teaspoon chili powder
- 1/4 teaspoon salt
- 1 minced garlic clove
- 1 teaspoon basil
- 1 cup chopped tomatoes
- 3/4 cup shredded cheddar cheese, seasonally optional
- 1 cup Italian style dressing or mayonnaise
- lettuce to preference
- 3-4 cups homemade corn chips
- 2 cups cooked kidney or black beans
- 3/4 cup chopped cucumbers, optional
- 1/2 cup chopped avocado, optional

Combine all ingredients, except chips and chill. Add chips just before serving. Serves 6.

Arroz con Frijoles

Cuban Rice and Beans
- 1 slice green bell pepper
- 1 chopped onion
- 2 minced garlic cloves
- 1/4 cup oil
- 2 cups cooked black beans with liquid
- 3 cups cooked brown rice

Heat oil and sauté pepper, onions and garlic. Mash beans slightly in their liquid and heat with the pepper mixture. Add vegetables and serve over rice. Serves 4.

Red Beans and Rice

New Orleans style—traditionally served on Monday.

- 2 1/2 cups dry red beans
- 9 c. water
- 1 bay leaf
- 2 teaspoons soy sauce
- 1 chopped onion
- 1 minced garlic clove
- 1 chopped celery stalk
- 1/4 teaspoon turmeric
- 1/2 teaspoon cumin
- 3/4 tsp. coriander
- 3 tablespoons oil
- 4 cups cooked brown rice

Add beans to water and boil. Reduce heat and add bay leaf and soy sauce. Separately heat oil and sauté vegetables and seasonings 3 minutes. Add to beans and simmer covered for 2 1/2 hours. Discard bay leaf and serve over rice. Serves 6. Good to do in a crock pot.

Zucchini Stuffed Mushrooms

- 1 lb. zucchini
- 1/4 teaspoon salt
- 2 lbs. large mushrooms
- 1/4 cup melted butter
- 1 minced garlic clove
- 1 minced tomato, optional
- 3/4 cup ricotta or cottage cheese
- 3/4 cup breadcrumbs
- 1 tablespoon fresh minced oregano, or dried equivalent
- 1/4 cup Parmesan cheese, seasonally optional

Shred zucchini and toss with salt in a colander. Place over a bowl for 30 minutes and let drain. Squeeze dry. Meanwhile, remove mushroom stems and brush them with all but 1 tablespoon of butter. Sauté garlic in reserved butter for 1 minute, then add zucchini for 2 minutes longer. Remove and stir in tomatoes, cheeses, crumbs and oregano. Spoon zucchini mixture into the mushrooms and place on baking sheet. Bake at 375° for 15 minutes. Serves 10.

Tamale Pie

Jones Family Favorite
- 2 cups cooked preferred bean
- 1/2 cup minced onion
- 1/2 cup chopped green bell pepper
- 1 chopped tomato
- 1/4 cup diced olives, optional
- 1 minced garlic clove
- 1 teaspoon cumin
- 1-3 teaspoons chili powder
- 1 teaspoon oregano
- 1 cup shredded cheddar cheese
- 1 recipe cornbread

Simmer beans, vegetables and seasoning with a little liquid for 10 minutes in a skillet. Stir in half the cheese. Prepare cornbread and pour half the batter into a greased 10-inch pie plate or 8-inch square dish. Add bean mixture on top, and top with remaining cornbread batter. Bake at 425° for 15 minutes. Top with remaining cheese and bake 10 minutes longer. Serves 6.

Squashed Nuts Casserole

- 1 lb. summer squash or zucchini, sliced
- 1/4 cup softened butter
- 1/4 cup chopped green bell pepper
- 1 tablespoon honey
- 1/2 cup chopped onion
- 1 egg
- 1/2 cup mayonnaise
- salt and pepper to taste
- 1/2 cup shredded cheddar cheese
- 1/2 cup chopped pecans
- 1/2 cup breadcrumbs

Steam squash until tender and drain. Add butter and mash. Add the bell pepper, honey, onion, egg, mayonnaise, salt, pepper, cheese and nuts. Transfer to a casserole dish and top with breadcrumbs. Dot with butter if desired. Bake at 350° for 40 minutes. Serves 8-10.

White Corn Tortilla Soup

By far, my family's favorite recipe in here.

- 3 tablespoons olive oil
- 1 1/2 seven-inch corn tortillas, cut into strips or 1-inch quarters
- 1 1/2 tablespoons minced fresh garlic
- 2 tablespoons minced white onion
- 1 lb. white corn kernels
- 1 1/2 lb. chopped, ripe red tomatoes
- 3/4 cup tomato paste
- 2 1/2 tsp, ground cumin
- 1 tablespoon salt
- 1/8 teaspoon ground white pepper
- 1/2 teaspoon chili powder
- 1 1/2 cup water
- 1 qt. stock
- homemade tortilla chips or fried tortilla strips, optional garnish
- 2 cups shredded cheese alternative, optional garnish
- 1/2 cup chopped fresh cilantro, garnish

Easily doubled and/or frozen. Over medium high heat, fry tortilla squares in oil until they begin to crisp. Add garlic and onion and cook 1-2 minutes, until onion becomes translucent. Add half the corn and all other ingredients, except garnishes. Bring the soup to a simmer for 5 minutes. Process in batches in a processor or blender to purée. Return soup to stove and add reserved corn. Serve with garnishes. Really is not complete without the cilantro and chips.

Wherefore it shall come to pass, if ye hearken to these judgments, and keep, and do them, that the Lord thy God shall keep unto thee the covenant and the mercy which he swore unto their fathers: And he will love thee, and bless thee, and multiply thee: he will also bless the fruit of thy womb, and the fruit of thy land...Thou shalt be blessed above all people: there shall not be male or female barren among you, or among your cattle.

Deut. 7:12-15

Summer Sides and Breads

Apple Date Bread

- 1/2 cup honey
- 1 1/2 cup milk or alternative
- 1 beaten egg
- 1 teaspoon vanilla
- 3 cups wheat flour
- 1 tablespoon baking powder
- 1 teaspoon salt
- 1 teaspoon cinnamon and nutmeg, optional
- 1 cup shredded coconut
- 1 cup minced apples
- 1 cup chopped dates

Combine honey, milk, egg and vanilla. Separately, mix the flour, powder, salt, cinnamon and nutmeg, then add to honey mixture. Fold in coconut, apples and dates. Pour into a greased and floured loaf pan and bake at 350° for 50 minutes. Serves 6.

Banana Nut Bread

- 1 3/4 cup wheat flour
- 1 teaspoon baking soda
- 1/2 teaspoon salt
- 3/4 cup oil
- 1/2 cup honey
- 2 beaten eggs
- 1 cup (3 medium) over ripe mashed bananas
- 1/4 cup hot water
- 1/2 cup chopped nuts, optional

Combine flour, soda and salt. Separately, combine the oil and honey. Add the eggs and bananas to the oil and honey. Add the dry ingredients, alternately with hot water, mixing well after each addition. Fold in nuts. Pour into a greased loaf pan and bake at 325° for 1 hour. Serves 6.

Sweet Cornbread

- ♦ 1 cup yellow cornmeal (preferably fine ground)
- ♦ 1 cup any type grain flour or wheat germ
- ♦ 1/2 teaspoon salt
- ♦ 2 teaspoons baking powder
- ♦ 4 tablespoons melted butter or oil
- ♦ 1-2 eggs
- ♦ 1 cup milk or alternative
- ♦ 4-6 tablespoons maple syrup, honey or molasses

Combine cornmeal, flour, salt and baking powder. Mix the butter, eggs, milk and maple syrup in a medium bowl. Add dry ingredients. Moisten, but do not overbeat. Pour into a greased 8 inch square pan. Bake at 400° for 20 minutes. Serves 8.

Summer Squash Rolls

- ♦ 3 3/4 cup wheat flour
- ♦ 1 tablespoon yeast
- ♦ 3 tablespoons honey
- ♦ 1 teaspoon salt
- ♦ 1/4 cup oil
- ♦ 1 cup grated yellow squash
- ♦ 3/4 cup milk or alternative
- ♦ 1 egg
- ♦ 2 teaspoons fresh dill weed

Combine 1 1/2 cup flour, yeast, honey and salt. Heat oil, squash and milk in a saucepan to approximately 120°. Pour into flour mixture and add egg and dill weed, stirring until a dough forms. Add enough remaining flour to make a soft dough. Knead for 5 minutes and let rise 1 1/2 hours. Punch down and divide into 24 balls. Place into two greased 8-inch round pans and let rise 45 minutes. Bake at 375° for 20-30 minutes.

Masa

For making corn tortillas.
- ◆ 2 lb. dried whole corn kernels, with enough water to cover
- ◆ 3 cups cold water
- ◆ 1/4 cup baking soda

In a non-aluminum pan, cover kernels with water that has the baking soda added to it by 2 inches. Boil, then simmer covered 2-3 hours (either on the stove or in a crock pot) until skins peel off. Remove from heat and add 3 cups cold water. Remove skins and rinse under cold running water until water runs clear. Now you have hominy. Grind in a processor until fine and light. This is masa flour. 4.5 cups of this makes 20 tortillas. Can be frozen.

Corn Tortillas

- ◆ 2 cups masa flour
- ◆ 1 3/4 cup water

Combine masa and water in a bowl, mixing quickly with fingers. Cover with a clean, damp towel and set aside. Preheat skillet until very hot. Do not grease. Shape dough into 8 balls. Roll from center outward between two sheets of wax paper or use a tortilla press. Peel off top sheet of waxed paper, place tortilla on hot skillet and remove remaining waxed paper. Cook for 1 minute each side. Repeat with remaining balls.

Corn Tortillas II

- ◆ 1 cup wheat flour
- ◆ 1 cup masa or cornmeal
- ◆ 3/4 teaspoon salt
- ◆ 2 tablespoons oil
- ◆ 2/3 cups warm water

Knead all ingredients. Divide into 12 balls. Roll out and cook as instructed in previous recipe.

Tropical Compote

♦ 2 star fruit, sliced crosswise (to form the star)
♦ I peeled, seeded and sliced thick papaya
♦ I peeled and sliced thick mango
♦ I 1/2 cup seedless grapes
♦ 2 sectioned oranges
♦ 1/4 cup lime juice
♦ 2 tablespoons apple juice

Arrange fruit on a platter and drizzle with lime and apple juice or combine all ingredients in a bowl. Bake at 350° for 15-20 minutes.

Stuffed Onions

♦ 4 large Vidalia or Spanish onions
♦ 1/2 cup stock
♦ I 1/4 cup steamed collard greens
♦ I teaspoon oregano
♦ 1/4 cup crumbled feta or blanched tofu
♦ 2 tablespoons breadcrumbs
♦ olive oil for rubbing

Preheat oven to 450° and lightly oil a baking dish. Peel the onions and chop off a slice at each bottom so they can sit in a baking dish. Use a melon baller to scoop out the insides of each onion, taking about 1/2 cup from each one. Chop the scooped out portions and add with the stock to a large skillet and simmer 5 minutes. Purée onions in a blender or processor, add greens, oregano, cheese and breadcrumbs while the motor is running and blend until smooth. Pack this into the hollowed onions, rub the outside with oil and set in prepared baking dish. Bake 20-25 minutes.

Corn Chips

- 2 cups corn kernels (3-4 ears)
- 3 tablespoons chopped green pepper, optional
- 3 tablespoons chopped tomato, including peel and seeds, optional
- 1/2 cup minced onion
- 1 minced garlic clove

Purée corn, onion and garlic in a blender or processor. Put plastic wrap over a cookie sheet and tape corners down. Pour corn mixture over it, spreading 1/4 inch thick, making an 8 x 13 inch rectangle. Sprinkle with pepper and tomato. Dehydrate 8-10 hours overnight, until crispy and crinkled. Break into chips. Makes 1 cup or more.

Corn Relish

- 1 cup cider vinegar
- 3/4 cup honey
- 1 teaspoon mustard seeds
- 1/2 teaspoon celery seeds
- 1/2 teaspoon turmeric
- 1/2 teaspoon salt
- 1/4 teaspoon dill seeds
- 1/4 teaspoon black pepper
- 1/2 cup chopped green bell pepper
- 1/2 cup chopped red bell pepper
- 1/2 cup chopped celery
- 3/4 cup chopped onion
- 3 cups packed corn kernels (5-6 ears)

Boil vinegar, honey, mustard seeds, celery seeds, turmeric, salt, dill seeds and black pepper in 3 qt. saucepan, then simmer 5 minutes. Add bell peppers, celery and onion. Return to boil, then simmer 10 minutes. Add corn and simmer 10 minutes longer. Pack into jars. Makes 3 1/2 cups.

Wild Rice and Endive Salad

- 1/4 cup sliced almonds
- 2 cups cooked wild rice
- 1 cup sliced fennel or celery
- 1 cubed endive
- 1/2 cup chopped dried figs
- 1 thinly sliced small red onion
- 3 tablespoons oil'
- 2 tablespoons lemon juice
- 1 tablespoon white vinegar
- 1/2 minced garlic clove
- leaf lettuce, optional

Toast almonds in a dry skillet and set aside. Combine rice, fennel, endive, fig and onion in a large bowl. Separately, combine oil, lemon juice, vinegar and garlic. Toss with the rice and serve over lettuce, topped with almonds. Serves 4.

Indian Rice

A Bene Israel Jewish Dish.

- 3 tablespoons oil
- 1 thinly sliced onion
- 1 3/4 cup basmati or long grain rice, soaked in cold water 30 minutes
- 10 oz. spinach leaves, steamed and squeezed dry
- 2 peeled and diced medium tomatoes
- 1/4 teaspoon turmeric
- 3/4 tsp. coriander plus 1/4 teaspoon cumin or 1 teaspoon dhana jeera
- salt and pepper to taste

Heat oil in a large saucepan and sauté onion 5-7 minutes. Add drained rice and cook 2 minutes. Add spinach, tomatoes, turmeric and coriander and cumin (or dhana jeera). Pour in 2 cups water and bring to a boil. Simmer covered 25 minutes. Fluff rice with a fork, being careful not to disturb the bottom layer, which will have formed a crust. Cover and cook on low 10 minutes and spoon into a serving dish, arranging the crisp rice around the rice. Serves 6.

Wild Rice with Apricots and Pecans

- ◆ 2 teaspoons butter
- ◆ 1 diced onion
- ◆ 2 diced seasonal carrots, opt.
- ◆ 1/2 cup wild rice
- ◆ 2 1/4 cup stock
- ◆ 1/2 cup preferred rice
- ◆ 1/2 cup chopped and toasted pecans
- ◆ 5 or more quartered apricots

Heat butter and sauté onions and carrots 5 minutes. Stir in wild rice and stock. Boil, then simmer covered 45 minutes. Add additional rice and boil again. Simmer covered 20 minutes or until rice is tender. Stir in pecans and apricots and heat through. Serves 8.

Sweet and Sour Sauce

- ◆ 1 cup pineapple chunks
- ◆ 1 cup pineapple juice
- ◆ 1/2-1 cup ketchup, opt.
- ◆ 3 tablespoons wine vinegar
- ◆ 1 tablespoon soy sauce
- ◆ 1 teaspoon mustard, opt.
- ◆ 1 teaspoon salt
- ◆ 1/8 teaspoon cayenne pepper, optional
- ◆ 1 minced green pepper
- ◆ 1 tablespoon flour
- ◆ 2 tablespoons cold water

Combine all ingredients and simmer 20 minutes. Makes 2 cups.

Corn and Black Bean Salad

- ◆ 3 cups corn kernels
- ◆ 2 cups cooked black beans
- ◆ 1 1/4 cup chopped tomato
- ◆ 3 tablespoons thinly sliced green onion
- ◆ 2 tablespoons chopped fresh cilantro
- ◆ 3 tablespoons olive oil
- ◆ 2 tablespoons lime juice
- ◆ 1/2 teaspoon salt

In a large bowl combine corn, beans, tomato, onion and cilantro. Separately whisk the oil, juice and salt together. Toss with vegetables. Serves 4.

Summer Desserts

Frozen Pineapple Yogurt

+ 1 1/2 cup chopped pineapple
+ 1 sliced banana
+ 2 cups plain yogurt
+ 2 tablespoons maple syrup

Purée pineapple and banana in a blender or processor. Stir in yogurt and maple syrup. Either put in an ice cream maker or freeze the mixture in a shallow dish. For the first 2 hours, stir or beat every 15-20 minutes to break up ice crystals and prevent it from freezing solid. Then allow to set in freezer 30-60 minutes.

Banana Ice Milk

+ 1 sliced banana
+ 1 1/2 cup milk or alternative
+ 2 tablespoons honey
+ 1 teaspoon vanilla
+ 1/8 teaspoon cinnamon

Purée bananas with 1/2 cup milk, honey, vanilla and cinnamon in a blender or processor. With motor running slowly add remaining milk. Either put in an ice cream maker or freeze the mixture in a shallow dish. For the first 2 hours, stir or beat every 15-20 minutes to break up ice crystals and prevent it from freezing solid. Then allow to set in freezer 30-60 minutes.

Strawberry Sherbet

- ◆ 2 cups sliced strawberries
- ◆ 1 cup orange juice
- ◆ 3 tablespoons honey
- ◆ 1 tablespoon lemon juice
- ◆ 2 cups honeydew balls

Purée strawberries, orange juice, honey and lemon juice in a blender or processor. Either put in an ice cream maker or freeze the mixture in a shallow dish. For the first 2 hours, stir or beat every 15-20 minutes to break up ice crystals and prevent it from freezing solid. Then allow to set in freezer 30-60 minutes.

Passion Fruit Freeze

- ◆ 7 ripe passion fruit
- ◆ 2 tablespoons orange juice
- ◆ 1 tablespoon lime juice
- ◆ 1 cup plain yogurt

Slice tops off of passion fruit and spoon out flesh into a blender or processor. Add orange juice and lime juice and process until smooth. Fold in yogurt. Either put in an ice cream maker or freeze the mixture in a shallow dish. For the first 2 hours, stir or beat every 15-20 minutes to break up ice crystals and prevent it from freezing solid. Then allow to set in freezer 30-60 minutes.

Lemon Berry Ice Cream

- ◆ 1 1/2 pt. fresh preferred berries
- ◆ 1/2 cup honey
- ◆ 1/4 cup lemon juice
- ◆ 1/2 teaspoon lemon zest
- ◆ 1 cup milk or alternative

Combine all ingredients in a processor or blender and puree. Either put in an ice cream maker or freeze the mixture in a shallow dish. For the first 2 hours, stir or beat every 15-20 minutes to break up ice crystals and prevent it from freezing solid. Then allow to set in freezer 30-60 minutes.

Cinnamon Peach Cobbler

- ◆ 2 egg whites
- ◆ 1/4 cup maple syrup
- ◆ 1 tablespoon oil
- ◆ 3/4 cup buttermilk or alternative
- ◆ 1/2 cup wheat pastry flour
- ◆ 2 tablespoons baking powder
- ◆ 3 cups (2 lbs.) peeled and sliced peaches
- ◆ 1 teaspoon cinnamon
- ◆ 1 teaspoon flour

Combine egg whites, maple syrup, oil and milk in medium bowl. Separately combine flour and baking powder and mix with egg mixture, but do not over mix, about 12 strokes. In another bowl combine peaches, cinnamon and flour. Pour into lightly oiled 8-inch square baking dish. Spread batter evenly over the peach mixture and bake at 375° for 20 minutes.

Fruity Grain Salad

- ◆ 1 1/2 cup cooked bulgar, quinoa or millet
- ◆ 1 diced cantaloupe or honeydew
- ◆ 1/2 cup halved grapes
- ◆ 1/2 cup raspberries
- ◆ 1/2 cup chopped pecans
- ◆ 1/2 cup chopped artichoke heart, water chestnuts or jicama
- ◆ 4 tablespoons oil
- ◆ 2 tablespoons lemon juice
- ◆ 1 tablespoon honey
- ◆ 1 teaspoon mustard, combined with honey
- ◆ salt and pepper to taste

Toss grain, melon, grapes, raspberries, pecans and artichoke in a large bowl. Separately, combine oil, lemon juice, honey, salt and pepper in a small bowl. Toss with the salad.

Rhubarb Pie

- ◆ 4 cups chopped rhubarb
- ◆ 3/4 cup raisins
- ◆ 1/2 teaspoon cinnamon
- ◆ salt to taste
- ◆ 2 1/2 tablespoons flour
- ◆ 3/4 cup honey
- ◆ homemade pie crust

Combine everything but the pie crust. Spoon into pastry lined pie plate and top with remaining pastry. Cut steam vents. Bake at 400° for 35-40 minutes

Banana Cream Shake

- ◆ 1 tablespoon apple juice
- ◆ 2 very ripe sliced and frozen bananas
- ◆ 1 teaspoon vanilla
- ◆ 1/2 cup cold or frozen seasonal fruit, such as peaches, strawberries or blueberries
- ◆ honey, if fruit is tart

Combine all ingredients in a blender or processor and purée until smooth. Serve immediately. Serves 4.

Banana Cake

- ◆ 1 3/4 cup wheat flour
- ◆ 3/4 cup wheat germ
- ◆ 1 cup honey or maple syrup
- ◆ 1 1/4 teaspoon baking powder
- ◆ 1 1/2 teaspoon baking soda
- ◆ 1 teaspoon salt
- ◆ 2/3 cups softened butter
- ◆ 2/3 cups buttermilk or alternative
- ◆ 2 eggs
- ◆ 1 1/2 cup mashed bananas
- ◆ 3/4 cup chopped pecans
- ◆ desired frosting or glaze

Combine all ingredients in a large mixing bowl. Blend until combined and then beat fast for 3 minutes. Pour into greased and floured 9 x 13 cake pan. Bake at 350° for 50 minutes. Top with frosting or glaze recipe. Serves 15.

Banana Barley Cookies

- ♦ 1 1/2 cup cooked barley
- ♦ 3 bananas
- ♦ 1 tablespoon vanilla
- ♦ 1 cup dates
- ♦ 3/4 cup water
- ♦ 1 cup chopped walnuts

Combine all ingredients except nuts, in a blender and process. Then add walnuts and place by the tablespoonfulls on a cookie sheet and bake at 350° for 8-12 minutes or dehydrate at 100° for 8-10 hours, turning after 4 hours.

Strawberry Pie

No bake and soooo good!

- ♦ 7-8 large quartered strawberries
- ♦ 5 pitted, soft chopped dates
- ♦ 2 mashed bananas
- ♦ 1 tablespoon lemon juice

pie shell (below)

Combine all ingredients and pour into the pie shell. Decorate with additional strawberries and chill.

No Bake Pie Shell

- ♦ 1 cup almonds
- ♦ 1 cup soft, pitted dates
- ♦ 1/2 teaspoon vanilla

Grind nuts in a blender or processor, add dates and vanilla and blend well. Press into the pie plate.

Peanut Butter Clusters

- ♦ 1 cup peanut butter
- ♦ 2 tablespoons honey
- ♦ 3 tablespoons butter
- ♦ 1 cup rolled oats
- ♦ 1/2 cup shredded coconut
- ♦ 1/2 cup raisins, optional
- ♦ wheat germ, optional

Mix peanut butter, honey and butter until smooth. Add oats, coconut and raisins. Drop by the rounded teaspoonful close together onto a cookie sheet. Roll in additional coconut and wheat germ. Freeze or refrigerate until set.

Peach Pie

No Bake

- ♦ 1/2 cup pecans, soaked in water 8-12 hours or overnight
- ♦ 5 ripe white peaches
- ♦ 1/2 cup chopped dried pineapple
- ♦ 3/4 cup chopped fresh pineapple
- ♦ 1/2 teaspoon cinnamon, optional
- ♦ 2/3 cups pitted soft dates
- ♦ 1 1/2 cup fresh berries for garnic, optional
- ♦ pie shell from strawberry pie recipe

Drain and rinse soaked pecans and set aside. Peel and halve peaches, reserving skins. Remove pit and slice thinly. Combine peach skins with pecans, dried and fresh pineapples, cinnamon and dates in a blender or processor and purée. Layer half the sliced peaches fan-style in the pie shell. Evenly spread 1/2 the pineapple mixture over the peach slices. Repeat with remaining peach slices and pineapple mixture. Garnish with reserved berries and chill.

Maple Popcorn

Jones Family Favorite

- ◆ 1/4 cup popping corn
- ◆ 1/2 teaspoon salt
- ◆ 1 cup maple syrup
- ◆ 1 1/2 teaspoon butter

Pop the corn and season with salt. Heat syrup and butter in saucepan, stirring constantly until temperature reaches 250°, or when a few drops of sauce form soft balls when dropped in cool water. Pour over popcorn and toss. May form balls.

"Prepare to die, is not the exhortation of this Church and Kingdom; but prepare to live is the word with us, and improve all we can in the life hereafter, wherein we may enjoy a more exalted condition of intelligence, wisdom, light, knowledge, power, glory and exaltation. Then let us seek to extend the present life to the uttermost, by observing every law of health...Let us teach these principles to our children, that in the morning of their days, they may be taught to lay the foundation of health and strength and constitution and power of life in their bodies."

Discourses of Brigham Young
compiled by John A. Widtsoe
(Salt Lake City: Deseret Book Company, 1977)
p 186

Recipe Favorites

Milk, Eggs, Bluefish, Rabbit, Turkey, Monkfish, Red Snapper, Salmon, Squid, Swordfish, Tuna, Apple, Cantaloupe, Cranberry, Fig, Grape, Honeydew, Mango, Nectarine, Orange, Peach, Pear, Persimmon, Pomegranate, Plum, Quince, Raspberry, Watermelon, Tomato, Broccoli, Brussels Sprouts, Cauliflower, Cabbage, Carrots, Eggplant, Fennel, Green Bean, Kale, Leek, Lettuce, Okra, Onion, Parsnip, Pepper, Potato, Beet, Bok Choy,

Fall

Fall Breakfasts

Date Nut Muffins

- ♦ 1 1/2 cup boiling water
- ♦ 1 1/2 cup chopped dates
- ♦ 1 egg
- ♦ 2 tablespoons oil or butter
- ♦ 3/4 cup wheat germ
- ♦ 2 teaspoons baking powder
- ♦ 1/2 cup chopped pecans or walnuts

Pour water over dates in a small bowl. Beat egg with oil in a medium bowl. Add wheat germ, baking powder and flour. Add dates and pecans, stirring until moistened. Fill greased muffin cups 2/3 full and bake at 400° for 15-20 minutes. Yields 16 muffins.

Orange Muffins

- ♦ 4 cups wheat flour
- ♦ 2 tablespoons baking powder
- ♦ 1 teaspoon salt
- ♦ 1 1/2 teaspoon cinnamon
- ♦ 2 eggs
- ♦ 1/2 cup oil
- ♦ 1/2 cup honey
- ♦ 2 tablespoons grated orange peel
- ♦ 2 cups orange juice

Combine flour, baking powder, salt and cinnamon in a large bowl. Separately combine eggs, oil, honey, orange peel and juice in a medium bowl. Add to dry ingredients, stirring until moistened. Fill greased muffin cups 2/3 full. Bake at 400° for 20 minutes. Yields 24 muffins.

Apple and Oat Bars

+ 1 1/3 cups rolled oats
+ 3/4 cup raw sunflower seeds
+ 1/2 teaspoon cinnamon
+ 2/3 cups dried apples
+ 2/3 cups puffed rice cereal
+ 1/2 cup maple syrup
+ 3 tablespoons pear or apple butter
+ 1 tablespoon butter

Put oats and seeds in a dry 9 x 13-inch pan and toast in 325° oven for 20 minutes. Remove and combine with cinnamon, dried apples and puffed rice in a large bowl. Boil the maple syrup, pear or apple butter and butter in a small saucepan, then simmer 5 minutes until syrup has thickened. Pour syrup over the dry ingredients, stirring quickly until well coated. Transfer to a lightly oiled 8-inch square cake pan and press down firmly. Bake 25 minutes at 325°, then cool completely and cut into 1 x 2-inch bars. Keeps in an airtight container for up to one week.

Sweet Pumpkin Cornbread

+ 2 teaspoons oil
+ 3/4 cup honey
+ 2 eggs
+ 2 teaspoons vanilla
+ 1 cup mashed cooked pumpkin
+ 1/4 cup cornmeal
+ 2 teaspoons baking powder
+ 1/2 teaspoon salt

Combine oil, honey, eggs and vanilla. Stir in pumpkin. Combine cornmeal, baking powder and salt separately. Add to pumpkin mixture. Pour into greased 5 x 9-inch loaf pan and bake at 350° for 40 minutes.

122

Potato and Pepper Saute

Late Fall dish.
- ♦ 6 cups peeled and diced red potatoes
- ♦ 2 cups diced onions
- ♦ 1 1/2 cup diced green bell pepper
- ♦ 1 1/2 cup diced red bell pepper
- ♦ 2 tablespoons oil
- ♦ 1 1/2 tablespoons minced garlic
- ♦ 1/4 cup minced fresh parsley
- ♦ 1 teaspoon thyme
- ♦ salt and pepper to taste

Sauté potatoes, onion and peppers in the oil 7-10 minutes. Then add the garlic and sauté 2 minutes longer. Add remaining spices and sauté 2 more minutes. Serves 6-8.

Fall Lunches

Red Beans and Barley

Jones Family Favorite
- ♦ 1 tablespoon olive oil
- ♦ 2 chopped onions
- ♦ 3 minced garlic cloves
- ♦ 1 seeded and minced jalapeno, optional
- ♦ 1 tablespoon chili powder
- ♦ 1 teaspoon oregano
- ♦ 2 cups chopped tomatoes
- ♦ 1 cup stock
- ♦ 2 cups cooked kidney beans
- ♦ 1 1/2 cup cooked barley

Heat oil in a soup pot on medium high. Sauté onion, garlic, jalapeno, chili powder and oregano 5 minutes. Add tomatoes, stock and beans and bring to a boil. Simmer covered 15 minutes. Serves 4.

Rice, Corn and Lentil Salad

- 2 teaspoons oil
- 2 diced carrots
- 1 diced red pepper
- 1 topped, tailed and thinly sliced leek
- 3/4 cup uncooked brown rice
- 1/4 cup dried lentils
- 2 cups stock or water
- 1 bay leaf
- 2 teaspoons oregano
- 1 cup corn kernels
- salt to taste

Heat oil in a large soup pot and sauté carrots, bell pepper and leek 2 minutes. Add rice and lentils and sauté 2 more minutes. Add stock and bay leaf and boil. Simmer covered 30 minutes. Add salt, oregano and corn. Serves 4.

Barley "Risotto"

- 1 cup uncooked barley
- 1 teaspoon olive oil
- 2 minced carrots
- 2 topped, tailed and minced leeks
- 2 minced garlic cloves
- 1 bay leaf
- 3 tsp. fresh rosemarry or dried equivalent
- 3 cups stock
- salt to taste

Heat barley on medium high in a large soup pot until toasted. Add oil, carrots, leeks, garlic, bay leaf and rosemary and sauté 3 minutes. Add salt and stock, bring to a boil. Simmer covered 35 minutes. Serves 4.

Wheat Berry Tomato Salad

- ◆ 2 cups cooked wheat
- ◆ 2 cups chopped tomatoes
- ◆ 1/2 cup chopped red onion
- ◆ 1/4 cup loosely packed basil leaves
- ◆ 2 tablespoons olive oil
- ◆ 1 tablespoon red wine vinegar
- ◆ 1/2 minced garlic clove
- ◆ salt and pepper to taste

Toss wheat, tomatoes and onion in a large bowl. Purée basil, oil, vinegar, garlic, salt and pepper in a blender or processor. Pour over salad. Serves 6.

California Salad

- ◆ 1 1/2 cup cooked millet
- ◆ 1/2 cup corn kernels
- ◆ 1 cup chopped celery
- ◆ 1 cup diced avocado
- ◆ 1/2 cup chopped red bell pepper
- ◆ 1 tablespoon minced scallion or onion
- ◆ 2 1/2 tablespoons lime juice
- ◆ 2 tablespoons olive oil
- ◆ 1/4 teaspoon grated lime zest
- ◆ 1/4 teaspoon celery seeds
- ◆ 1/8 teaspoon ground red pepper
- ◆ salt to taste

Toss millet, corn, celery, avocado, red bell pepper and scallion in a large bowl. Separately, combine remaining ingredients and pour over millet and toss. Serves 8.

Fruity Quinoa Salad

Jones Family Favorite

- ◆ 1/2 cup slivered almonds
- ◆ 2 oranges
- ◆ 2 cups cooked quinoa
- ◆ 1/2 cup chopped green bell pepper
- ◆ 3/4 cup minced onion
- ◆ 1 tablespoon oil
- ◆ 3 tablespoons orange juice
- ◆ 1 teaspoon cider vinegar
- ◆ 1 teaspoon honey
- ◆ 1 teaspoon mustard
- ◆ lettuce leaves, optional

Toast almonds in a small dry skillet and set aside. Grate 1 tablespoon orange zest. Peel the rind and the bitter white membrane beneath it. Cut oranges in a shallow dish into 1/4-inch slices, reserving accumulating juice; add additional orange juice to equal 3 tablespoons Toss quinoa, green pepper, onion and almonds in a large bowl. Separately, combine oil, orange juice, vinegar, honey, mustard, orange slices and rind. Toss with quinoa. Line plates or serving bowl with lettuce leaves, then top with the salad. Serves 4-6.

Waldorf Salad

Excellent

- ◆ 2 cups rice or similar grain
- ◆ 1 minced onion
- ◆ 6 stringed and diced celery stalks
- ◆ 4 minced scallions
- ◆ 1/2 cup chopped walnuts
- ◆ 1 chopped red apple
- ◆ 1 choppled green apple
- ◆ 2/3 cups mayonnaise
- ◆ 3 tablespoons minced fresh parsley
- ◆ juice of one lemon

Combine all ingredients and mix well. Serves 4-6.

Jicama Salad

- 1 large jicama, peeled and julienned
- 2 cups Jerusalem artichoke, julienned
- 1 bunch chopped watercress
- 4 diced green onions
- 1 medium red bell pepper, julienned
- 1 diced garlic clove
- 1 tablespoon oil
- 1/4 cup cider vinegar
- 1/4 cup spicy mustard
- 1 teaspoon diced fresh dill
- 2 sprigs fresh diced parsley
- 2 sprigs chopped cilantro
- black pepper to taste

Combine all ingredients and mix well. Cover and marinate 1 hour.

Tuna and Bean Salad

Tuscan Genius

- 3/4 cup cooked and shredded tuna
- 3 cups cooked white beans
- 3/4 cup minced red onion
- 1 tablespoon lemon juice
- 2 teaspoons fresh oregano, or dried equivalent
- 1/4 teaspoon pepper
- 3 tablespoons olive oil
- 1/2 cup chopped fresh Italian parsley, or dried equivalent
- salt to taste
- 3 tomatoes, cut in wedges

Combine beans, onion and tuna in a large bowl. Separately, combine the lemon juice, oregano and pepper, then whisk in oil until blended. Toss with the beans and refrigerate 1 hour. Season with salt and parsley when ready to serve and arrange the tomatoes around the salad. Serves 4.

Broccoli Walnut Sandwich Roll

- 2 teaspoons olive oil
- 1 small slivered onion
- 2 minced garlic cloves
- 2 1/4 cup chopped broccoli
- 1/4 cup water
- 1 cup shredded cheddar cheese
- 1/2 cup toasted and chopped walnuts
- 1/4 cup Parmesan cheese
- 1 lb. bread dough

Sauté onions in oil for 2 minutes. Add garlic, broccoli and water and simmer covered 5 minutes. Uncover and cook 1 minute until water evaporates. Remove and stir in cheese, walnuts and Parmesan, then cool. Roll dough on a floured surface to a 12 x 12-inch square. Spread cooled filling down the center of the dough in a 3 1/2-inch strip, to within one inch of each end. Fold ends over filling, then fold in sides and pinch to seal. Roll onto a greased baking sheet so loaf is seam side down. Bake at 400° for 30 minutes. Remove to a wire rack and cool 15 minutes, then slice. Serves 8-12.

Six Layer Casserole

- 1 cup cooked brown rice
- 1 cup cooked soy or other bean
- 1 cup sliced onion
- 1 chopped green bell pepper
- 1 cup grated carrot
- salt and pepper to taste
- 1 teaspoon basil
- 2 cups tomato juice
- 2 tablespoons Worcestshire sauce
- 1 cup shredded sharp cheddar cheese
- 1/4 cup wheat germ, optional

Layer rice, beans, onion, bell pepper and carrots in oiled 3 qt. casserole dish, sprinkling with salt and pepper. Combine basil, tomato juice and Worcestshire sauce. Pour over layers. Top with cheese and wheat germ and bake covered at 350° for 1 1/2 hours. Serves 8.

Tuscan Bread Salad

Great Party Dish

- 3/4 cup chopped fresh basil, or dried equivalent
- 3 minced garlic cloves
- 6 quartered tomatoes
- 1 thinly sliced red onion
- 1 day old, crust bread loaf, cubed
- 3/4 cup homemade balsamic vinaigrette
- salt and pepper to taste

Combine vinaigrette, onion, basil and garlic. Pour over cubed bread and tomatoes, then toss well. Season with salt and pepper. Cover and chill 1 hour. Serves 4-6.

Quinoa Melody

- 2 cups cooked quinoa
- 6 minced green onions
- 1 grated carrot
- 1 diced cucumber
- 4 tablespoons minced
- fresh parsley
- 2 tablespoons fresh mint
- 4 tablespoons lemon juice
- 3 tablespoons olive oil

Combine everything but the lemon juice and oil. Separately combine the juice and oil. Pour over salad and toss. Serves 4.

"Almost daily we read of those who invest for little return. We eat food so refined that the nourishment is lacking. We witness the drink that can never satisfy the thirst for those who drink; the dressing for style rather than for warmth, comfort, and modesty; the high wages of the wage earner today which still do not satisfy or supply his needs."

Elder L. Tom Perry
"Consider Your Ways",
The Ensign, July 1973, p. 20

Fall Dinners

Stuffed Acorn Squash

+ 2 large acorn squash
+ 1/2 cup chopped onion
+ 1/2 cup diced celery, seasonally optional
+ 1/2 cup sunflower seeds
+ 2 minced garlic cloves
+ 2 tablespoons oil
+ 1 cup breadcrumbs
+ 1/4 cup raisins
+ 2 tablespoons lemon juice
+ 2 teaspoons fresh sage, or dried equivalent
+ 2 teaspoons fresh thyme, or dried equivalent
+ 1/4 teaspoon black pepper
+ 1/2 cup shredded cheddar cheese

Halve squash lengthwise and discard seeds. Heat oil in a large skillet and sauté onions, celery, garlic and sunflower seeds 5 minutes. Add breadcrumbs, raisins, lemon juice, sage, thyme and pepper, then simmer 5 minutes. Remove from heat and mix in cheese. Pack the stuffing into the squash cavities. Grease a 9 x 13-inch baking dish and add the squashed. Bake at 350° for 30 minutes until tender.

Bean Burgers

+ 1 1/2 cup cooked black eyed peas or black beans
+ 3 tablespoons fresh thyme or dried equivalent
+ 2 tablespoons minced red bell pepper
+ 1/4 cup minced onion
+ salt and pepper to taste

Purée peas in a blender or processor. Add remaining ingredients and mix well by hand. Heat skillet on medium high. Form pea mixture into 10 patties. Brown each patty about 2 minutes each side. Serve as you would hamburgers.

Bean Burritos

♦ 1 tablespoon olive oil
♦ 1 minced onion
♦ 1 minced garlic clove
♦ 4 chopped and roasted bell peppers
♦ 1 1/2 cup cooked pinto beans
♦ 2 seeded and minced hot peppers, optional
♦ 3 teaspoon fresh oregano, or dried equivalent
♦ 4 whole grain flour tortillas
♦ 1/2 cup ricotta or cottage cheese

Heat oil on medium high in a large skillet. Sauté onion and garlic 5 minutes. Add peppers, beans and oregano and sauté 2 more minutes. Warm tortillas in a separate skillet. Spread 1/4 cup of the filling down the center of each tortilla. Top with 1 tablespoon of cheese. Turn one end in, fold on long side over the filling and roll up. Set the tortilla in a warm baking dish in the oven while you repeat with the rest of the tortillas.

Barley and Beans

Tasty and Easy
♦ 2 tablespoons oil
♦ 1/2 cup chopped onion
♦ 1 cup chopped bell pepper
♦ 1 3/4 cup water
♦ 1 cup tomato sauce, optionally seasoned with jalapeno
♦ 1/4 teaspoon cumin
♦ 1/8 teaspoon oregano
♦ 1 cup uncooked barley
♦ 1 cup cooked pinto or kidney bean

Heat oil in a 2 qt. saucepan and sauté onion and bell peppers 4 minutes. Add water, tomato sauce, cumin and oregano and boil. Add barley and simmer covered 40 minutes. Stir in beans and simmer 5 minutes longer. Serves 4.

Fall Casserole

- 1 cup cooked millet
- 1 cup diced butternut squash
- 1/2 cup chopped walnuts
- 1/2 cup apple juice
- 1/4 cup cranberries
- 4 tablespoons honey
- 1 teaspoon cinnamon

Combine all ingredients in a 1 1/2 qt. casserole dish and bake covered for 40 minutes. Serves 6.

Grain Stuffing

Makes 3.5 cups.

- 1/2 lb. cleaned and chopped mustard greens and preferred greens
- 2-4 tablespoons oil
- 1 chopped onion
- 1/2 celery stalk, chopped
- 3/4 cup chopped green bell pepper
- 2 minced garlic cloves
- 1 cup stock
- 2 teaspoons mustard
- salt, pepper, cumin and cayenne to taste
- 3/4 cup toasted slivered almonds
- 2 2/3 cups cooked grain or rice
- 2 chopped scallions

Make sure greens are free from all debris and thoroughly dried. Heat oil in a skillet and sauté greens 5 minutes. Remove and set aside. In another skillet, heat more oil and sauté onion, celery, green bell pepper and garlic 5 minutes. Add stock and spices and cook until slightly reduced. Add greens, almonds, rice and scallions. Use as you would regular stuffing.

"...we are told that flesh of any kind is not suitable to man (in) the summer time, and ought to be eaten sparingly in the winter."

Journal of Discourses 12:221-222

Meatless Sloppy Joes

♦ 2 tablespoons oil
♦ 1 cup minced onion
♦ 1 chopped green bell pepper
♦ 2 minced garlic cloves
♦ 1 1/2 teaspoon chili powder
♦ 1 tablespoon fresh thyme or dried equivalent
♦ 4 large chopped tomatoes
♦ 1 juiced tomato
♦ 2 cups cooked red beans
♦ 1 tablespoon ketchup
♦ 1 tablespoon cider vinegar

Heat oil in a large skillet and sauté onion and green bell pepper 5 minutes. Add garlic, chili powder and thyme. Add tomatoes, juice, beans and 1/2 cup water. Boil, chunking up the tomatoes. Simmer covered 15 minutes. Mash a quarter of the beans against the side of the pan. Add the ketchup and vinegar and simmer uncovered until thickened, adding water to prevent sticking to the pan if necessary. Spoon on rolls or buns. Serves 4.

"The Americans, as a nation, are killing themselves with their vices and high living. As much as a man ought to eat in half an hour they swallow in three minutes, gulping down their food like the canine quadruped under the table, which, when a chunk of meat is thrown down to it, swallows it before you can say 'twice.'...Dispense with your multitudinous dishes, and depend upon it, you will do much towards preserving your families from sickness, diseases and death...it would add ten years to the lives of our children. That is worth a great deal."

Journal of Discourses 13:154

Feijoada

Brazilian Rice and Beans
- ◆ 4 cups cooked black beans
- ◆ 1 tablespoon fresh chopped oregano, or dried equivalent
- ◆ 1 teaspoon salt
- ◆ 2 minced garlic cloves
- ◆ 3 chopped tomatoes
- ◆ 2 chopped onions
- ◆ 2 tablespoons oil
- ◆ 1 cup cooked sausage or ham, optional

Mix the beans, oregano, salt, 1 clove garlic and meat. Heat oil and sauté remaining garlic, tomatoes and onion. Add 1/3 cup of the bean mixture and mash. Add remaining bean mixture. Serve over rice (below). Serves 8. Traditionally served with oranges and cooked greens.

Feijoada Rice
- ◆ 1 chopped onion
- ◆ 2 chopped tomatoes
- ◆ 2 minced garlic cloves
- ◆ 3 tablespoons oil
- ◆ 2 1/2 cups uncooked brown rice
- ◆ 5 cups boiling water

Heat oil in a pot and sauté onion garlic and tomatoes. Add rice and boiling water and simmer 45 minutes.

And there were some who died with fevers, which at some seasons of the year were very frequent in the land but not so much so with fevers because of the excellent qualities of the many plants and roots which God had prepared to remove the cause of diseases, to which men were subject by the nature of the climate.

Alma 46:40

Vegetable Pie

Southwest Style
- ◆ oil for frying
- ◆ corn tortillas
- ◆ I cup (5 oz.) sesame seeds
- ◆ 1/2 cup hulled, raw pumpkin seeds
- ◆ 3/4 cup shelled pistachio nuts
- ◆ 3/4 cup almonds
- ◆ 4 garlic cloves
- ◆ 3 chopped poblano chiles
- ◆ 4 chopped serrano chiles
- ◆ I 1/2 cup (1/2 lb.) chopped tomatillos
- ◆ 2 cups fresh cilantro
- ◆ I cup shredded lettuce
- ◆ 4 cups stock
- ◆ 3 tablespoons oil
- ◆ 2 lb. seasonal vegetable, chopped and sauteed
- ◆ grated cheese

Fry tortillas in small amount of oil. Transfer to a paper towel to drain. In a dry skillet, toast the sesame seeds about 8 minutes. Remove and cool. Toast pumpkin seeds in the same dry skillet until they puff up but do not darken, 2-3 minutes. Add pumpkin seeds along with pistacho and almonds. Purée garlic, chiles, tomatillos, cilantro, lettuce and 2 cups stock until thickened. Add seed-nut mixture and purée until smooth. Heat oil in a large saucepan and add mixture. Add remaining broth and simmer 12 minutes until thickened. Stir in half the vegetables and simmer 10 minutes. Line tortillas in the bottom of a pie plate, add half the sauced vegetables, top with cheese and repeat with remaining tortillas, sauced vegetables and cheese. Bake at 350° for 20 minutes. Slice and serve.

Chile Quinoa Casserole

- oil
- 2 1/2 cups cooked quinoa
- 1 minced garlic clove
- 1 bunch chopped scallions
- 1 diced onion
- 2 cups chopped tomatoes
- 2 cups cooked pinto beans
- 1 1/2 teaspoon cumin
- 1/2 teaspoon salt
- 1 tablespoon chopped fresh oregano, or dried equivalent
- 1/2 teaspoon chili powder
- 4 whole grain flour tortillas
- 1/2 cup green chiles, cut into strips
- grated cheese
- 1 bunch chopped fresh cilantro

Heat oil in a large skillet and sauté garlic, scallions and onion. Add tomatoes, pinto beans, cumin, salt, oregano and chili powder and simmer 5 minutes. Grease 9 x 13-inch pan and arrange tortillas in the bottom and top with tomato mixture. Cover with quinoa and green chile strips. Cover and bake at 325° for 25 minutes. Sprinkle with cheese and cilantro. Bake an additional 5 minutes. Serves 6-8.

German Rice Salad

- 3/4 cup (6 1/2 oz.) flaked tuna
- 1 minced onion
- 3 chopped hard-boiled eggs
- 1 chopped large dill pickle
- 1 chopped green bell pepper
- 1-3 tablespoons oil
- 1-2 tablespoons vinegar
- 2 cups cooked brown rice
- 3 chopped large tomatoes

Combine tuna, onion, eggs, pickle and bell pepper in a bowl. Add oil and vinegar. Stir in rice and tomatoes. Chill before serving. Garnish with tomato, lemon wedges and parsley. Serve with breadsticks or rolls. Serves 8.

Corn and Cabbage Skillet

- 1 1/2 cup corn
- 2 cups shredded cabbage
- 2 tablespoons chopped onion
- 2 tablespoons butter
- 1/2 cup cottage cheese
- 1/4 cup plain yogurt or sour cream
- 2 tablespoons Parmesan
- 1/2 teaspoon salt
- dash of pepper

Steam corn and cabbage 7 minutes. Heat butter and sauté onion until soft. Add remaining ingredients, except corn and cabbage, stirring until cheese begins to melt. Combine with the corn and cabbage. Serves 6.

Cheese Enchiladas

- 3 tablespoons oil
- 1 tablespoon chili powder
- 2 tablespoons flour
- 2 cups water or stock
- 1 teaspoon vinegar
- 1 minced garlic clove
- 1 tablespoon fresh chopped oregano
- salt to taste
- 2 cups cooked pinto beans
- 1/4 cup chopped green onions
- 1 cup cottage or sharp cheddar cheese
- 1 cup shredded cheddar cheese
- 8 corn tortillas

Optional:

- 1/2 cup chopped green bell pepper
- 1/4 cup chopped onions
- 1/2 cup wheat germ
- 1/2 cup chopped olives

Combine oil, chili powder, flour, water, vinegar, garlic, oregano and salt and heat in a saucepan. Combine beans, onions, cottage or shredded sharp cheese, bell pepper, wheat germ and olives. Mash the beans up as you combine. Briefly fry tortillas in oil, spoon filling and roll. Place seam side down in a casserole dish and top with cheddar cheese. Bake at 320° for 20 minutes.

Rice and Black Eyed Pea Salad

- 1 chopped onion
- 2 teaspoons olive oil
- 2/3 cups uncooked brown rice
- 1 3/4 cup water
- 3/4 tsp. grated lemon rind
- 1/4 teaspoon salt
- 2 1/2 cups cooked black eyed peas, black beans or lima beans
- 3 cups salad greens
- 1 large chopped tomato

Sauté onion in oil 6 minutes. Add rice to coat 1 minute. Add water, lemon and salt. Boil, then simmer covered 15-25 minutes. Transfer to a bowl and add beans. Add the dressing (below). Arrange greens on a platter and spoon the salad on top, then sprinkle with tomato. Serves 6.

Dressing

- 1 large (9 oz.) peeled and chopped tomato
- 2 tablespoons olive oil
- 1 tablespoon red wine vinegar
- 1/4 teaspoon salt
- 1 teaspoon chopped fresh oregano, or dried equivalent

Combine ingredients in a blender and processor and purée 1 minute.

"I believe that we enslave our women;...our tables are covered with every delicacy and variety that we can think of...I do not believe in mixing up our food. This is hurtful. It destroys the stomach by overtaxing the digestive powers; and in addition to that it almost wears out the lives of our females by keeping them so closely confined over cooking stoves...We can have a variety in diet, and yet have simplicity. We can have a diet that will be easily prepared, and yet have it healthful. We can have a diet, that will be tasteful, nutritious and delightful to us, and easy to digest...."

Journal of Discourses 13:154

Mashed Potato and Roasted Vegetable Enchiladas

Soooo good!

- 1 chopped broccoli head
- 1 cup chopped mushrooms
- 1-1 1/2 cup chopped seasonal squash
- 2 cups chopped carrot
- 4 cups homemade mashed potatoes
- 3 cups homemade enchilada sauce
- 1 cup shredded cheddar cheese
- 12 corn or flour tortillas
- olive oil
- salt and pepper to taste

Combine broccoli, mushrooms, squash and carrots. Drizzle with olive oil and season with salt and pepper. Spread vegetables in a single layer in a jellyroll pan and roast at 425° for 30-40 minutes, stirring halfway. Reduce to 350° when done. Combine potatoes and vegetables. Heat tortillas in a pan to make pliable. Dip tortillas in enchilada sauce and then place a large spoonful – 1/3-1/4 cup – of the potato mixture down the center of each tortilla. Sprinkle with cheese and roll. Place seam side down in baking dish. Pour extra enchilada sauce over the top and sprinkle with remaining cheese. Bake at 350° for 30 minutes. Serves 6.

Cream of Broccoli Soup

- 1 lb. chopped broccoli
- 1/2 cup water
- 1/2 lb. butter
- 1 cup flour
- 1 qt. stock
- 1 cup half and half, whole milk or alternative
- 1 teaspoon salt
- 1/2 teaspoon pepper

Steam broccoli in 1/2 cup water until al dente, reserving water. Separately whisk flour into stock, add butter and heat until melted. Simmer and add the broccoli, milk, salt and pepper, making sure not to boil. Serves 4-6.

Broccoli, Potato & Leek Soup

- ◆ 1 tablespoon oil
- ◆ 3/4 lb. chopped broccoli
- ◆ 1 large chopped potato
- ◆ 2 chopped shallots
- ◆ 1 minced garlic clove
- ◆ 2 cups stock or water
- ◆ 2 teaspoons fresh thyme, or equivalent
- ◆ 2 teaspoons fresh oregano, or dried equivalent
- ◆ 2 teaspoons mustard
- ◆ 1 cup milk or alternative
- ◆ 1/4 cup feta cheese
- ◆ salt to taste

Heat oil in large stock pot and sauté broccoli, potato, leek, shallots and garlic 5 minutes. Add 1 cup stock or water, thyme and oregano and simmer covered 20 minutes. Cool soup and purée in processor or blender. Don't over process. Pour this back into the soup pot and add remaining stock, milk, cheese and salt and warm through. Serves 2.

Split Pea Soup

Not Your Mama's Split Pea Soup

- ◆ 2 cups dried (uncooked) split peas
- ◆ 10 cups stock
- ◆ 2 minced garlic cloves
- ◆ 1 chopped onion
- ◆ 2 chopped celery stalks, including leaves
- ◆ 4 chopped carrots
- ◆ 2 chopped large potatoes
- ◆ 1 bay leaf
- ◆ 1 tablespoon fresh rosemary
- ◆ salt and pepper to taste

Boil split peas and stock in large pot. Add the remaining ingredients and simmer covered 1 1/2 hours, or in a crockpot on high. Serves 10.

Grain Vegetable Soup

- 1 chopped onion
- 1 tablespoon oil
- 3 cups stock
- 2 diced carrots
- 1 diced celery stalk
- 1 chopped zucchini
- 1 cup sliced green beans
- 1 diced tomato

- 1 bay leaf
- 2 teaspoons fresh thyme
- 2 teaspoons fresh basil, or dried alternative
- 1 cup shredded spinach
- 1 cup cooked preferred grain
- 1 cup milk or alternative

Heat oil in 3 qt. saucepan and sauté onion 3 minutes. Add stock, potato, carrots, celery, zucchini, beans, tomato, bay leaf, thyme and basil and simmer covered 30 minutes. Stir in spinach, grains and milk. Simmer covered 5 minutes and discard bay leaf. Serves 4-6.

Pumpkin Bisque

- 1 small pumpkin (2 1/2 lbs.)
- 2 tablespoons oil
- 1 grated carrot
- 2 medium onions

- 1 minced garlic clove
- salt to taste
- 5 cups stock
- 1 tomato

Slice off the top and bottom of the pumpkin and set it upright. From top to bottom, cut off the skin as you would peel an orange. Cut the pumpkin in half and scoop out the seeds. Cut into 1 1/2-inch chunks. Heat oil in a large pot and sauté carrots, whole onions and garlic for 10 minutes. Add pumpkin, stock and salt and bring to a boil. Drop the whole tomato in for 30 seconds, then remove to peel off skin. Cut the tomato in half and squeeze out seeds and discard skin. Mince the tomato and add it to the soup. Simmer uncovered 30 minutes. Remove and purée in blender or processor until smooth. Return to pot and reheat. Serves 8-10.

Sweet Squash Bisque

- 1 chopped onion
- 1/2 large chopped leak
- 2 tablespoons oil
- 5 lb. butternut squash, peeled, seeded and chopped
- 3/4 gallon stock
- 2 chiles, seeded and torn into large pieces, optional
- 1/2 cup honey
- 2 tablespoons fresh chopped sage, or dried equivalent
- 2 tablespoons fresh chopped thyme, or dried equivalent
- salt and pepper to taste
- cilantro for garnish

Heat oil in a large stock pot and sauté leek. Add squash and simmer covered 1 hour. Toast chiles in a hot skillet. Add to soup during simmer. Stir in honey, sage, thyme, salt and pepper. Purée, in batches if necessary, in a processor or blender. Garnish with Maple Cream (below) and cilantro. Serves 8.

Cinnamon Maple Cream

- 1/2 cup sour cream
- 1/2 teaspoon lime juice
- 1 teaspoon maple syrup
- 1/2 teaspoon cinnamon

Combine thoroughly.

Behold, verily, thus saith the Lord unto you: In consequence of evils and designs which do and will exist in the hearts of conspiring men in the last days, I have warned you, and forewarn you, by giving unto you this word of wisdom by revelation.

D&C 89:4

Fall Sides and Breads

Carrot Bread

- ◆ 1 1/2 cup wheat flour
- ◆ 1/2 teaspoon baking powder
- ◆ 1/2 teaspoon baking soda
- ◆ 1/2 teaspoon salt
- ◆ 1 1/2 teaspoon cinnamon
- ◆ 1/2 cup oil
- ◆ 1/2 cup honey
- ◆ 2 beaten eggs
- ◆ 1 teaspoon vanilla
- ◆ 1 1/2 cup grated carrot
- ◆ 1/2 cup chopped walnuts

Combine flour, soda, powder, salt and cinnamon. Separately beat honey and oil in a large bowl. Add eggs, vanilla and carrot. Stir in dry ingredients, fold in walnuts. Pour into a greased loaf pan. Bake at 350° for 45-60 minutes. Serves 6.

Rye Bread

Czech-Bohemian

- ♦ 4 cups warm water
- ♦ 1 1/2 tablespoons honey
- ♦ 1 tablespoon salt
- ♦ 1 1/2 teaspoon caraway seeds
- ♦ 1 1/2 cup wheat flour
- ♦ 2 1/2 cups rye flour
- ♦ 2 sliced potatoes
- ♦ 2 tablespoons butter
- ♦ 2 tablespoons oil
- ♦ 3 1/4 cup wheat flour
- ♦ 3 1/4 cup rye flour

Combine the water, honey, salt and yeast in a large bowl. Add the seeds. Combine 1 1/2 cup wheat flour and 2 1/2 cups rye flour and add to yeast mixture with a wooden spoon. Let rise 1 hour. Cook potato slices until tender, drain and mash with butter and oil, and add to yeast mixture. Stir in remaining flours and beat with a wooden spoon 15 minutes. This will take the place of kneading. Dough should be elastic. Let rise 1 hour. Stir down and let rise again 30 minutes. Divide into 3 portions, kneading each portion briefly and adding flour if necessary. Place in greased loaf pans and let rise 45 minutes. Do not over rise. Bake loaves at 350° for 1 hour 15 minutes. Turn oven off, remove from pans and let stand in oven 20 minutes.

> "Man requires food to build up his body. He requires food that is adapted to the development of bone, muscle and sinew; but this is not all. He requires food that is suitable to feed his brain and to supply the waste sustained in consequence of the use of his mental faculties."
>
> *Elder George Q. Cannon*
> *Journal of Discourses 12:221-222*

Pumpkin Cornbread

- 1/4 cup butter
- 1 chopped onion
- 1 cup yellow cornmeal
- 2/3 cups flour
- 1 tablespoon baking powder
- 1/2 teaspoon baking soda
- 3/4 teaspoon salt
- 1/4 teaspoon pepper
- 4 tablespoons honey or maple syrup
- 1 cup pureed pumpkin
- 2 beaten eggs
- 3/4 cup buttermilk

Sauté onion in 1 tablespoon butter 5 minutes. Combine corn-meal, flour, baking powder and soda, salt and pepper in a large bowl. Separately, combine honey, pumpkin, eggs, buttermilk and onion. Place remaining 3 tablespoons butter in a 9 x 9-inch baking dish and place in warmed oven until melted, swirl to coat pan. Pour remaining butter in pumpkin mixture, then add the cornmeal to the pumpkin mixture. Pour into buttered dish and smooth the top. Bake at 400° for 25-30 minutes.

Cranberry Pears

- 8 firm pears
- 1 tablespoon lime juice
- 2 cups cranberries
- 1 cup pear juice
- 2 tablespoons honey
- 1/2 teaspoon cinnamon
- 1/8 teaspoon cloves

If desired, peel the pears, leaving stems intact. Using a melon scoop, core the pears from the bottom and brush with lime juice. Arrange upright in a shallow baking dish. Combine cranberries and pear juice in a saucepan and cook until cranberries pop, about 5 minutes. Add honey, cinnamon and cloves and pour over pears. Bake at 350° for 30 minutes.

Baked Onions with Pumpkin

- ♦ 2 1/2 lb. jack-o-lantern type pumpkin
- ♦ 2 chopped onions
- ♦ 1 chopped apple
- ♦ pinch of cinnamon and salt

Cut the top off the pumpkin and use a large spoon to scrape out and discard or reserve seeds for toasting. Fill the pumpkin with the onions, apples, cinnamon and salt and stir. Replace the pumpkin top, covering the stem with foil. Set the pumpkin on a baking dish and bake at 375° for 2 hours. Open the pumpkin and serve, making sure to scoop some of the pumpkin with the onions and apple.

Hot Pepper Salsa

- ♦ 1 teaspoon fresh minced cilantro
- ♦ 2 chopped and roasted bell peppers
- ♦ 1-2 minced garlic cloves
- ♦ 1-2 fresh seeded hot peppers
- ♦ 1/2 teaspoon cumin
- ♦ 2 teaspoons fresh oregano
- ♦ 1/2 teaspoon honey
- ♦ 1 tablespoon balsamic vinegar
- ♦ salt to taste

Purée all ingredients in a blender or processor until slightly chunky. Yields 2 cups.

Poor Man's Caviar

+ 1 1/2 lb. eggplant
+ 1/4 cup oil
+ 3/4 cup minced onion
+ 1/2 cup minced green pepper
+ 3 minced garlic cloves
+ 1 1/2 cup chopped tomato
+ 3/4 cup cooked amaranth
+ 3 tablespoons water
+ 1 teaspoon white vinegar
+ salt and pepper to taste

Bake eggplant at 400° for 1 hour. Meanwhile, heat oil in a large skillet and sauté onion, green pepper and garlic 4 minutes. Add tomato and simmer 15 minutes, then remove from heat. Cut eggplant in half and scrape the flesh out of the shell; chop finely. Stir into skillet mixture and simmer 20 minutes. Add remaining ingredients and cook until thickened. Makes 2 3/4 cups. Serve with water crackers or vegetables.

Rice Cakes

+ 2 cups cooked rice or similar grain
+ 1 beaten egg
+ 2 teaspoons fresh parsley
+ 1 finely chopped tomato
+ 1 finely chopped bunch of chives
+ 2 tablespoons oil for frying
+ 2 tablespoons thyme
+ sour cream, optional

Combine rice, onion, parsley, tomato, chives and thyme. Form into 6 patties. Heat oil in a skillet on medium high and fry the patties until browned on both sides. Drain on a paper towel and garnish with parsley and sour cream dollops.

Green Chile Sauce

- 3 1/2 lb. roasted, peeled and diced green chiles
- 1 lb. diced tomatoes
- 1 lb. diced onions
- 1/2 minced garlic clove
- 1 1/2 tablespoons salt
- 1/2 tablespoons pepper
- 3 tablespoons fresh oregano
- 5 cups water
- 1/4 cup cold water
- 2 tablespoons flour

Combine chiles, tomatoes, onions, garlic, salt, pepper, oregano and 5 cups water in a 4 qt. pot. Boil, then simmer 90 minutes. Turn up heat until the sauce comes to a very slow boil. Mix the flour and 1/4 cup cold water to form a slurry. Turn the heat off under the sauce and immediately and slowly add the slurry while stirring rapidly. Pour into jars and freeze or refrigerate unused portion.

Quince Cups

- 4 large quinces
- 3 tablespoons honey
- 2 teaspoons lemon juice
- 1 cup apricots
- 2 tablespoons raisins
- 1 tablespoon olive oil
- 1/4 cup minced onions
- 1/2 cup cooked preferred grains
- 2 tablespoons toasted pine nuts
- 1/4 tablespoons allpsice
- salt to taste

Peel, halve and core the quinces. Hollow the core to make a cup and place cut side down in a baking dish. Combine honey and lemon juice and drizzle half of it over the quinces. Pour a little water to cover the bottom and keep the quinces from scorching. Bake at 350° for 30 minutes. Pour boiling water over the raisins and let them plump 15 minutes. Heat oil in a skillet and sauté the onion until soft, but not brown. Drop the raisins and combine with grains, onion, pine nuts, allspice and salt. Turn the quince halves over and spoon grain mixture into each cup. Drizzle remaining juice and honey mixture on top. Add a little more water to the pan and bake 30 minutes longer.

Green Bean Creole

- 1/4 cup chopped onion
- 1/4 cup chopped bell pepper
- 1 tablespoon oil
- 2 cups fresh green beans
- 1 cup chopped tomatoes
- 1/2 teaspoon salt
- dash of pepper
- 1 teaspoon each minced fresh marjoram and oregano, optional
- 1/2 cup grated cheddar cheese
- 1/2 cup breadcrumbs

Heat oil in a skillet and sauté onion and bell pepper. Mix with beans, tomatoes and seasonings. Spoon into a 2 qt. greased casserole dish and top with cheese and breadcrumbs. Bake at 350° for 20 minutes. Serves 5.

Indian Green Beans

- 1 lb. fresh green beans
- 2-4 tablespoons oil
- 1 teaspoon mustard seeds
- 1/2 cup chopped onion
- 3/4 cup thinly sliced carrots
- 3 tsp. fresh coriander
- 1/8 teaspoon ground ginger
- 1/2 teaspoon salt
- 1-2 tablespoons lemon juice

Cut beans into one each diagonal slices and set aside. Heat oil in a large skillet or wok and sauté the mustard seeds until they begin to pop. Add beans, onion and carrots and cook for 5 minutes, stirring constantly. Add seasonings and reduce heat and simmer covered 8-10 minutes. Stir in lemon juice. Serves 5.

Cranberry Sauce

- 2 cups cranberries
- 1 peeled & chopped orange
- 1 peeled & chopped apple
- 1 cup pitted dates
- water for consistency

Combine all ingredients and process in a blender or processor. Makes 4 cups.

Sweet and Sour Sauce

♦ I cup ketchup
♦ 1/2 cup soy sauce
♦ 1/4 cup orange juice
♦ 1/4 cup hoisin sauce
♦ 2 tablespoons brown rice syrup
♦ 2 tablespoons sesame oil

Whisk together. Yields 2 1/4 cups.

Cranberry, Orange and Raspberry Jam

♦ I cup dried or fresh cranberries
♦ 2/3 cups orange juice
♦ I teaspoon orange zest
♦ 1/4 cup brown rice syrup
♦ 2 cups raspberries or blackberries
♦ I teaspoon lemon juice

Heat the cranberries, juice, zest and brown rice syrup in a small saucepan for 5-7 minutes. Transfer to a blender or processor and add the remaining ingredients. Pulse to form a chunky puree. Transfer to a jar and chill covered for several hours to allow flavors to blend. Yields I cup.

Fall Desserts

Vanilla Poached Pears

♦ 2 large pears, halved and cored
♦ 2 cups apple juice
♦ I cinnamon stick
♦ I vanilla bean, slit vertically

Boil all the ingredients in a skillet. Simmer covered 20 minutes. Let pears relax in the juice about 10 minutes.

150

Pear Sauce

- ◆ 4 peeled, cored and chopped pears
- ◆ 6 dried apricots
- ◆ 1/2 cup orange juice

Boil all ingredients in a small saucepan, simmer 4 minutes, then cool 5 minutes. Purée in a blender or processor. Serve atop pancakes, grain cereal, fruit salad, yogurt or ice cream. Yields 5 cups.

Creamed Persimmon

- ◆ 2 halved persimmons
- ◆ 2 tablespoons fresh lemon, lime or orange juice
- ◆ 1/2 cup chilled heavy cream
- ◆ ground ginger, cinnamon or nutmeg for dusting

Scrape off persimmon pulp from the skin. Purée the flesh in a processor or blender or by pressing it through a sieve with a spoon. Whip the cream until it peaks and top the puree. Dust with spices. Serves 4.

Persimmon Pudding

- ◆ 2 halved persimmons
- ◆ 4 1/2 tsp lemon juice
- ◆ 1 cup flour
- ◆ 3/4 cup honey
- ◆ 1 teaspoon baking soda
- ◆ pinch of salt
- ◆ 1/2 teaspoon cinnamon
- ◆ 1/4 tsp ground ginger
- ◆ 1/2 cup milk
- ◆ 1/4 cup melted and cooled butter
- ◆ 3/4 cup toasted and chopped hazelnuts, or preferred nut

Butter and flour an 8-inch round cake pan. Scrape the persimmon flesh from the skins. Purée in a processor or blender, or press the flesh through a sieve with the back of a spoon to measure 1 cup. Add the lemon juice. Separately, combine the flour, soda, salt and spices. Stir the milk into the eggs, then add the butter and honey. Alternately stir the dry and moist ingredients into the persimmon. Finally, fold in the nuts. Pour the batter into the cake pan and bake at 350° for 50 minutes. Let the pudding cool and slice into wedges. Serves 6.

Pumpkin Walnut Pie

- ♦ 9-inch walnut pastry shell, unbaked
- ♦ 3 eggs
- ♦ 1 1/2 cup pureed pumpkin
- ♦ 1/2 cup maple syrup
- ♦ 1 cup heavy cream
- ♦ 3/4 tsp. cinnamon
- ♦ 1/2 teaspoon nutmeg
- ♦ 1/2 teaspoon grated ginger
- ♦ 1/4 teaspoon salt

Chill the pricked pastry shell, line with foil, weight it with dry beans or pie weights and bake at 425° for 10 minutes. Remove the foil and weights and bake for an additional 6 minutes. Remove and lower heat to 350°. Beat the eggs and pumpkin together, then stir in remaining ingredients. Pour the batter into the pie shell and bake at 350° for 35 minutes, until set around the edges and barely liquid in the center. Pie will solidify as it cools.

Pumpkin Bars

- ♦ 1/2 cup oil
- ♦ 3/4 cup honey or maple syrup
- ♦ 2 eggs
- ♦ 1 cup plus 2 tablespoons wheat flour
- ♦ 1 teaspoon baking powder
- ♦ 1/2 teaspoon baking soda
- ♦ 1 cup mashed cooked pumpkin
- ♦ 3/4 teaspoon cinnamon
- ♦ 3/4 cup chopped nuts
- ♦ homemade cream cheese frosting, optional

Combine all ingredients and spread in a greased 9 x 13-inch pan. Bake at 350° for 30 minutes. Cool and frost. Makes 36 bars.

Carrot Cake

- 1/2 cup grated carrot
- 1 1/4 cup chopped dates
- 1 3/4 cup water
- 1 cup raisins
- 1/4 cup butter
- 1 teaspoon each ground cinnamon, cloves and nutmeg
- 2 cups wheat flour
- 1 teaspoon baking powder
- 1 teaspoon baking soda
- 1/4 teaspoon salt
- 1/2 cup chopped walnuts

Boil carrots, dates, water, raisins, butter and spices in a saucepan and simmer 5 minutes. Mix flour, powder, soda and salt in a large bowl. Add carrot mixture with walnuts. Spoon into a greased 9-inch ring mold. Bake at 375° for 50 minutes. Serves 8.

> And again verily I say unto you, all wholesome herbs God hath ordained for the constitution, nature, and use of man.
>
> *D&C 89:10*

Pumpkin-Less Pie

No Bake

- ◆ 4 cups chopped carrots
- ◆ 3/4 cup almonds, soaked 12-48 hours
- ◆ 1/2 cup walnuts, soaked 6 hours and rinsed
- ◆ 2-4 tablespoons powdered psyllium husks,

optional
- ◆ 1 1/2 cup dates
- ◆ 2 teaspoons cinnamon
- ◆ 1 teaspoon grated ginger
- ◆ 1/4 teaspoon cloves
- ◆ 1 teaspoon vanilla
- ◆ Topping (below)

Process nuts, carrots and dates in a processor. Add spices and psyllium. Put into a pie plate and press firmly. Smooth the surface and refrigerate until firm enough to spread topping on.

Pumpkin-Less Pie Topping

- ◆ 1/2 cup chopped dates
- ◆ 1 cup almonds, soaked 12-48 hours
- ◆ 1 teaspoon cinnamon
- ◆ 1 teaspoon vanilla
- ◆ 1 tablespoon shredded coconut
- ◆ water for consistency

Process dates and almonds in a processor. Add vanilla and spread over pie. Dust with coconut and chill.

Avocado Dessert

No Bake

- ◆ 2 peeled and pitted avocados
- ◆ 1 cup seedless grapes
- ◆ 2 bananas
- ◆ 1 cup yogurt
- ◆ 2 tablespoons honey
- ◆ 3 tablespoons orange juice
- ◆ 1 tsp grated orange rind
- ◆ salt to taste
- ◆ 1 tablespoon lemon juice
- ◆ 2 tablespoons grated lemon rind

Chop avocados and combine with grapes. Slice banana and add. Whisk yogurt with remaining ingredients and pour over fruit. Garnish with mint. Serves 4-5.

Raspberry Slush

- 1/2 pt. red raspberries
- 1/2 cup white grape juice
- 1 teaspoon lemon juice
- 1 1/2 cup ice

Combine ingredients in a blender and whiz until slushy.

Apple Spice Cake

- 3 cups wheat flour
- 2 tablespoons baking soda
- 1 teaspoon baking powder
- 1 teaspoon cinnamon
- 1/4 teaspoon nutmeg
- 1/2 teaspoon cardamon, optional
- 1/4 teaspoon ground ginger
- 1/4 teaspoon salt
- 2 1/2 cups apple sauce
- 1 cup apple juice
- 2 tablespoons oil
- 1 teaspoon vanilla

Sift the flour, baking powder and soda and spice together. Separately combine the remaining ingredients together. Add the wet and dry ingredients together and mix. Pour batter into a greased 9 x 13-inch dish and bake at 350° for 30 minutes. Serves 12.

Pumpkin Mousse

- 4 eggs, separated
- 3/4 cup honey
- 2 cups (16 oz.) pumpkin puree
- 2 teaspoons flour
- 1 1/2 teaspoon cinnamon
- 1/4 teaspoon nutmeg
- 1/4 teaspoon salt

In the top of a double broiler, combine egg whites and honey; simmer until mixture reaches 160°. Transfer to a medium bowl and mix with an electric mixer on high speed until peaks form. In a medium saucepan combine yolks, pumpkin, flour, cinnamon, nutmeg and salt and cook until boiling, then remove from heat. Add 1/4 of the stiff egg whites, then gradually stir in the remaining whites. Spoon into dessert glasses, cover, chill 30 minutes or more, then serve. Serves 6.

Recipe Favorites

Milk, Eggs, Beef, Pig, Turkey, Apple, Avocado, Clementine, Cranberry, Grapefruit, Lemon, Orange, Tangerine, Pear, Pomegranate, Artichoke, Beet, Burdock, Cabbage, Carrots, Celeriac, Celery, Collard Greens, Daikon, Horseradish, Kale, Kohlrabi, Leek, Mushroom, Mustard Greens, Onions, Parsnip, Potato, Radish, Rutabaga, Shallot, Squash, Turnip

Winter

Winter Breakfasts

Carrot Spice Muffins

- 1 1/2 cup wheat flour
- 1 teaspoon baking soda
- 1 teaspoon baking powder
- salt to taste
- 1/2 teaspoon cinnamon
- 1/4 teaspoon nutmeg
- 1/8 teaspoon ground ginger
- 1/8 tsp allpsice
- 3/4 cup honey
- 1 egg
- 1/2 cup sour milk, buttermilk, yogurt, or alternative
- 3/4 cup oil or butter
- 1/2 teaspoon vanilla
- 1 1/2 cup grated carrot
- 1/2 cup raisins
- 1/2 cup chopped pecans or walnuts

Combine flour, soda, powder and spices in a medium bowl. Separately, combine honey, egg, milk, oil, vanilla, carrots, raisins and pecans in a large bowl. Add to dry ingredients and mix well. Fill greased muffin cups 2/3 full and bake at 400° for 15 minutes.

Apple Muffins

- 2 unpeeled, finely chopped apples
- 1/2 cup honey
- 1 beaten egg
- 1/4 cup oil or butter
- 1 cup milk or alternative
- 1 3/4 cup wheat flour
- 1/2 teaspoon cinnamon
- 1/2 teaspoon salt
- 2 teaspoons baking powder
- 1/4 cup wheat germ

Toss apples and honey in a bowl. Beat egg, oil and milk in a large bowl. Add flour, cinnamon, salt, baking powder and wheat germ. Fold in apple mixture. Fill greased muffin cups 2/3 full and bake at 400° for 20-25 minutes. Yields 16 muffins.

157

Apple Bread

- ◆ 2 cups wheat flour
- ◆ I teaspoon baking soda
- ◆ I teaspoon baking powder
- ◆ 1/2 teaspoon salt
- ◆ 1/4 cup oil
- ◆ 1/2 cup honey
- ◆ I tablespoon buttermilk
- ◆ 1-2 beaten eggs
- ◆ 2 cups grated apples
- ◆ 1-2 teaspoons vanilla
- ◆ I tablespoon cinnamon
- ◆ 1/2 cup chopped nuts, optional

Combine flour, soda, salt and powder. Separately, combine oil and honey. Stir in buttermilk and eggs. Add dry ingredients. Fold in apples and remaining ingredients. Bake at 350° for 45 minutes.

Apple Bread Topping

- ◆ 2 tablespoons butter
- ◆ 2 tablespoons flour
- ◆ 2 tablespoons honey
- ◆ I teaspoon cinnamon

Combine well.

Every herb in the season thereof, and every fruit in the season thereof, and these to be used with prudence and thanksgiving.

D&C 89:11

Apple Pecan Sticky Buns

- 1 cup milk or alternative
- 1/2 cup apple juice
- 2 tablespoons oil
- 3 tablespoons yeast
- 1/2 teaspoon salt
- 3-4 cups wheat flour
- 1 1/4 cup chopped pecans

- 1 1/2 cup peeled and chopped apples
- 2 teaspoons cinnamon
- 1/2 teaspoon coriander
- 1/4 teaspoon nutmeg
- 2/3 cups maple syrup
- 3 tablespoons honey

Heat milk until tiny bubbles form at edges. Transfer to a large bowl and add 1/3 cup of the apple juice and set aside to cool. When luke warm add 4 tablespoons oil, yeast and salt. Add 3 cups of the flour and stir into a dough, knead 5 minutes, adding additional flour if needed. Lightly oil the bowl the dough was in and return the dough. Move dough around so it gets oil on all sides and cover with a damp towel. Let rise until doubled, 45-55 minutes. Meanwhile, toast 1/2 cup of the pecans for 3 minutes in a dry skillet. Add the apples and cook until softened. Add 1/2 teaspoon cinnamon, coriander and nutmeg, cook an additional 2 minutes. Grease 9 x 13-inch dish and pour the maple syrup and remaining 2 tablespoons apple juice in the bottom. Sprinkle the remaining 3/4 cup pecans evenly over the bottom and set the dish aside. In a small bowl combine the honey and remaining 1 1/2 teaspoons cinnamon and set aside. After dough has doubled, punch it down and transfer it to a floured surface and knead 2 minutes. Roll out to a 9 x 13-inch rectangle, brush remaining 2 teaspoons oil over the dough, leaving a 1-inch border around the edge. Spread the apple-pecan mixture over the dough and drizzle the cinnamon-honey over that. Starting from the long side, roll up into a log and pinch the seams closed. Cut into 12 rounds and place side-up in the baking dish, making sure the rolls do not touch. Cover and let rest 15 minutes. Bake at 350° for 25 minutes. Place a large cookie sheet over the dish and carefully flip it. Allow the dish to remain on top 2 minutes so that the nuts will adhere. Yields 12 buns.

Winter Lunches

Buckwheat Pilaf with Garlic and Leeks

- 1 tablespoon oil
- 2 minced garlic cloves
- 2 diced carrots
- 1 minced leek
- 1 cup uncooked buckwheat
- 2 1/2 cups vegetable stock
- 2 minced scallions
- 1 teaspoon balsamic vinegar
- salt to taste

Heat oil in a medium saucepan. Sauté garlic, carrots, leek and buckwheat 5 minutes. Add stock and salt and boil, then simmer covered 45 minutes. Stir in scallions and vinegar. Serves 2-4.

Fajitas

- 1 lb. sliced raw meat or mushrooms
- 1/2 cup lime juice
- 2 tablespoons coriander
- 1 teaspoon oil
- 1 minced garlic clove
- 3/4 teaspoon cumin
- 1/4 teaspoon oregano
- 1/4 teaspoon black pepper
- 1 cup thinly sliced onions
- 3 sliced chile peppers, optional
- 1 cup diced tomatoes
- 6 flour tortillas

Combine 1/4 cup lime, coriander, oil, garlic, cumin, oregano and black pepper. Add meat or mushrooms. Cover and refrigerate 2 hours to marinate. Heat broiler and place meat or mushrooms on a greased cookie sheet, reserving marinade. Broil each side 4 minutes. Combine marinade, onions and chili peppers in a heated skillet and cook until tender, about 3 minutes. Add tomatoes and 1/4 cup lime juice, cook 3 minutes longer. Add meat or mushrooms. Divide among tortillas and add desired toppings.

WheatBerry Scampi

- 1/2 cup butter
- 4 minced garlic cloves
- 1 1/2 lb. peeled and cleaned shrimp
- 1/5 cups chopped fresh parsley
- 1 tablespoon lemon juice
- 1/4 teaspoon pepper
- 2 3/4 cups cooked wheat berries

Heat butter and sauté garlic and shrimp until cooked through. Add remaining ingredients and heat through. Serves 4-6.

O'Brien Potatoes

- 1 1/2 cup milk or alternative
- 1/2 cup butter
- 6 medium grated potatoes
- 1/2 chopped green bell pepper
- 1/2 chopped red bell pepper
- 5 sliced scallions
- 1/2 teaspoon salt

Heat milk and butter until butter melts. Layer potatoes, peppers and scallions in a greased 2 qt. dish, sprinkle with salt. Pour milk over the top. Bake at 275° for 2 hours. Serves 8.

All grain is...to be the staff of life, not only for man, but for the beasts of the field, and the fowls of heaven, and all the wild animals that creep on the earth; and these hath God made for the use of man only in times of famine and excess hunger.

D&C 89:14-15

Winter Salad

- 3 carrots
- 3 parsnips
- I leek
- 2 tablespoons olive oil
- I bell pepper, cut into strips
- head of winter lettuce

Shred or julienne the carrots and parsnips. Cut off the end and all but I inch off the top of the leek. Cut lengthwise into 2-inch slivers, then rinse. Sauté leeks in oil for 4 minutes, add carrots, parsnips and pepper and cook for 5 minutes. Add the honey mustard dressing below. Line salad plates with lettuce leaves and spoon salad in the center.

Honey Mustard Dressing

- 2 tablespoons red wine vinegar
- 2 tablespoons olive oil
- 2 teaspoons mustard
- I teaspoon honey
- 3/4 teaspoon salt

Whisk all ingredients together and refrigerate covered for at least 3 hours.

All grain is good for the food of man, as also the fruit of the vine; that which yieldeth fruit, whether in the ground or above the ground.

D&C 89:16

Potato and Onion Frittata

- ◆ 4 tablespoons butter
- ◆ 1/2 lb. (3 small) red potatoes, thinly sliced
- ◆ 1 chopped onion, preferably red
- ◆ 1 teaspoon minced or powdered rosemary
- ◆ 1 minced garlic clove
- ◆ 6 beaten eggs
- ◆ 3 tablespoons milk
- ◆ 1/2 teaspoon salt
- ◆ 1/4 teaspoon pepper

Heat 2 tablespoons butter in a skillet with an ovenproof handle (if not ovenproof, wrap handle in foil to protect it). Sauté potatoes 2-3 minutes, turning once halfway through cooking. Add onion and rosemary and sauté 3 minutes. Add garlic, sauté 2 minutes. Remove to a bowl and reduce heat to low. Add eggs to potatoes along with milk, salt and pepper. Melt remaining butter on the bottoms and sides of skillet. Pour in the mixture and cook, shaking pan back and forth, until frittata is firm on the bottom and almost set on top, 8-10 minutes. Remove and arrange several potatoes on top. Bake at 350° for 5-8 minutes, until eggs are set. Makes 6 wedges.

Whole Meal Salad

- ◆ 3 chopped hard-boiled eggs
- ◆ 1 diced sweet pickle
- ◆ 6 sliced radishes
- ◆ 1 cup diced or shredded meat, optional
- ◆ 2 cups cooked wheat
- ◆ 1 large shredded carrot
- ◆ 1/2 cup minced onion
- ◆ sprouts
- ◆ 1/2-1 cup preferred homemade salad dressings

Combine all ingredients and serve on winter lettuce. Serves 6.

Cream of Split Pea Soup

- ◆ 2 cups dry split peas
- ◆ 4 1/2 cup boiling water
- ◆ 1/2 cup chopped carrots
- ◆ 1 chopped onion
- ◆ 2 teaspoons salt
- ◆ 2 1/2 cups milk or alternative
- ◆ preferred herbs to taste
- ◆ chunks of preferred meat, optional

Combine water, peas, vegetables and salt in a large pot and simmer 45 minutes. Purée in a blender or processer. Add milk, seasonings and meat and reheat on stove. Serves 8.

Lima Bean Chowder

- ◆ 2 slices, diced and cooked bacon
- ◆ 2 small minced onions
- ◆ 4 medium diced potatoes
- ◆ 3 diced carrots
- ◆ 2 cups cooked lima beans
- ◆ 1 teaspoon salt
- ◆ 4 cups boiling water
- ◆ 2 cups milk or alternative
- ◆ 4 tablespoons flour
- ◆ 4 tablespoons butter

Brown onions in bacon grease, add cooked bacon, potatoes, carrots, beans and salt. Cover with boiling water and cook until tender, 45 minutes or more. Meanwhile, whisk the flour into the milk and add the butter. Boil, then simmer until thickened. Add remaining ingredients and flour to thicken if desired. Serves 6.

Basil Potato Soup

- 1 1/2 cup halved and quartered small red potatoes
- 1/4 cup fresh basil
- 1/4 cup sour cream
- 2 garlic cloves
- 3 tablespoons toasted almonds or pine nuts
- 3 tablespoons Parmesan
- 1/2 cup mayonnaise
- salt and pepper to taste

Boil potatoes until tender and set aside. In a blender or processor, chop the basil, add garlic and pulse until chopped. Add nuts and pulse again. Add remaining ingredients and blend well. Serves 4.

Beans and Greens

- 3 cups cooked black eyed peas
- 2 tablespoons oil
- 2 minced garlic cloves
- 2 bay leaves
- 1 bunch Swiss chard
- 1 tablespoon fresh minced thyme, or equivalent
- salt and pepper to taste

Sauté all ingredients, except peas and chard, 3 minutes. Add peas and chard and simmer 15-20 minutes. Season with salt and pepper.

Potato and Teff Latkes

- 1 cup cooked teff
- 1 cup shredded raw potato
- 1 egg
- 2 teaspoons grated onion
- 1/2 teaspoon salt
- pepper to taste
- oil for frying

Mash teff with the back of a spoon and combine with potato, egg, onion, salt and pepper. Pour 1/4 inch of oil in a large skillet and heat until bubbling. Drop batter into oil by the spoonful, then flatten with a spatula. Fry both sides until browned. Serve with applesauce or sour cream. Makes 15 latkes.

Curried Brown Rice

- ♦ 1 cooked brown rice
- ♦ 1 tablespoon curry
- ♦ 1 lb. carrots
- ♦ 1/2 small beet
- ♦ spinach and soaked flax seeds
- ♦ 1 minced garlic clove
- ♦ 1/2 minced onion
- ♦ oil
- ♦ mung bean sprouts, chopped

Combine rice and sprouts and place on a serving dish. Combine the onion and garlic in glass and cover with olive oil and let soak. Combine curry powder and enough oil to make a paste. Juice the beet, carrots and spinach. Add the curry paste and mix well. Serve the onion and garlic mixture, juiced curry mixture and rice separately, side by side. You take the desired amount of each dish to customize your taste. Serves 2-4.

Beet and Carrot Slaw

- ♦ 3 cups beets, peeled and grated
- ♦ 3 cups carrots, peeled and grated
- ♦ 3 cups shredded red cabbage
- ♦ 3/4 cup olive oil
- ♦ 3 tablespoons orange juice
- ♦ 3 tablespoons lemon juice
- ♦ 3 tablespoons snipped fresh chives, or dried equivalent
- ♦ salt and pepper to taste

Toss the beets, carrots and cabbage together. Add remaining ingredients and blend well. Chill for 1 hour. Serves 6-8.

Winter Dinners

Sweet Potatoes with Apples and Cinnamon

- ◆ 2 sliced sweet potatoes
- ◆ 2 sliced tart apples
- ◆ 1/2 cup apple juice
- ◆ 1 bay leaf
- ◆ 1/2 teaspoon cinnamon
- ◆ salt to taste

In a medium sized oven dish, combine all the ingredients and cover with foil. Bake at 375° for 45 minutes. May serve over rice. Serves 2-3.

Chick Pea and Potato Curry

East Indian Garbanzo Bean Dish

- ◆ 1 lb. cubed potatoes
- ◆ 1 sliced small onion
- ◆ 2 minced garlic cloves
- ◆ 1/2 cup chopped collards, kale or other hearty greens
- ◆ 1 cup cooked chick peas (garbanzo beans)
- ◆ 1 teaspoon curry
- ◆ 1 tablespoon lemon juice
- ◆ 4 tablespoons tomato sauce
- ◆ 1 tablespoon milk
- ◆ pinch of salt and nutmeg
- ◆ 1 cup cooked and cubed chicken, optional

Boil potatoes, onion, garlic, collards and chick peas for 15 minutes. Heat oil and sauté curry, nutmeg, lemon juice, tomato sauce and chicken. Pour over potato mixture, add milk and salt. Serves 2.

Italian Rice

- ◆ 5 cups vegetable stock
- ◆ 2 teaspoons olive oil
- ◆ 1 leek, topped, tailed and chopped
- ◆ 1 1/2 cup uncooked arborio rice
- ◆ 1/2 teaspoon saffron threads or curry powder
- ◆ 1 grated carrot
- ◆ 2 tablespoons Parmesan
- ◆ 2 scallions, or 1 onion, minced

Warm stock in a pot. Meanwhile heat a large skillet and add oil. Sauté the leek, carrot and rice about 3 minutes. Ladle enough stock to just cover the rice, add the saffron or curry, and simmer gently until rice has absorbed all the stock. Add another cup of stock and continue to stir and simmer. If the pan is too hot, the rice won't be creamy. Keep adding stock by the cupful until all 5 cups have been absorbed, about 25 minutes. Immediately toss in the cheese and scallions. You may just pour the entire 5 cups of stock over the rice, cover and let simmer 25 minutes, but the rice won't be as creamy and soft. Serves 4.

And all saints who remember to keep and do these sayings, walking in obedience to the commandments, shall receive health to their naval and marrow to their bones; and shall find wisdom and great treasures of knowledge, even hidden treasures. And shall run and not be weary, and shall walk and not faint. And I, the Lord,...promise, that the destroying angel shall pass by them...and not slay them.

D&C 89:18-21

Cabbage Rolls

+ 1/2 cup uncooked millet or preferred grain
+ 1 1/2 teaspoon oil
+ 1/2 cup grated carrot
+ 1/2 cup chopped onion
+ 1/2 cup Parmesan cheese
+ 1 teaspoon chopped fresh parsley, or dried equivalent
+ 8 large cabbage leaves
+ dash of cayenne

Heat oil in skillet and sauté millet 2-3 minutes. Add cayenne and water and simmer covered 35 minutes. Add carrot, onion, cheese and parsley. Spoon 2-3 tablespoons millet into each cabbage leaf and roll filling. Place seam side down on oiled baking dish. Pour sauce (below) over rolls and bake at 325° for 30 minutes. Serves 8.

Cabbage Roll Sauce

+ 1 cup sauced tomatoes
+ 2 teaspoons lemon juice
+ 1-2 tablespoons honey
+ 1/2 teaspoon allspice

Combine together.

Yea, flesh also of the beasts and fowls of the air, I, the Lord have ordained for the use of man with thanksgiving: nevertheless they are to be used sparingly; and it is pleasing until me that they should not be used, only in times of winter, or of cold, or famine.
D&C 89:12-13

Not Quite
Spaghetti and Meat Sauce

- 2 lbs. spaghetti squash, halved lengthwise
- 2 tablespoons olive oil
- 1 cup chopped onion
- 2 minced garlic cloves
- 1 3/4 cup whole peeled tomatoes
- 1/2 cup tomato sauce
- 1 bay leaf
- 3 teaspoons basil
- 2 teaspoons oregano
- 1/4 teaspoon honey
- 1/4 teaspoon salt
- 1/8 teaspoon pepper
- 1/4 cup minced fresh parsley, or dried equivalent
- 1 cup cooked bulgar

Discard squash seeds and place squash halves, cut side down, in a baking dish and bake 50 minutes at 375°. Meanwhile, heat oil in a 3 qt. saucepan and sauté onion until soft. Add tomatoes, breaking up with the back of a spoon. Add tomato sauce and spices. Boil, then simmer covered 20 minutes. Discard bay leaf and add bulgar. Remove squash and, using the tins of a fork, separate the spaghetti like strands as you scrape them from the shell. Place in a dish and top with sauce.

Barley and Veggie Bake

- 1/2 cup uncooked barley
- 1 cup one-inch cubed squash, preferably butternut
- 1 cup julienned carrots
- 1/2 cup julienned parsnips
- 1 1/2 cup boiling water
- 2 teaspoons honey
- 3/4 teaspoon salt
- 1/8 teaspoon nutmeg
- 2 tablespoons butter

Place barley in a 2 qt. casserole dish and arrange squash, carrots and parsnips evenly. Drizzle with water over it and sprinkle with salt, nutmeg and honey. Dot with butter. Bake covered for 1 hour at 350°. Stir to combine. Serves 6.

Potato Pie

- ◆ 1 tablespoon butter
- ◆ 2 large grated potatoes
- ◆ 1/2 teaspoon salt
- ◆ 1 cup shredded Swiss or cheddar cheese
- ◆ 1 chopped onion
- ◆ 2 beaten eggs
- ◆ 1 cup milk
- ◆ 2 teaspoons chopped fresh parsley, or dried equivalent
- ◆ 1/2 teaspoon pepper
- ◆ 1 tablespoon mustard

Press the grated potatoes into a greased 9-inch pie plate. Sprinkle with salt and cheese. Heat butter in a skillet and sauté onion, spread over cheese. Beat remaining ingredients in a bowl and pour over the onion. Bake at 375° for 45 minutes. Let stand 10 minutes. Serves 4-6.

Bubble and Squeak

My kids actually ate this one! It is very tasty.
- ◆ 1 chopped onion
- ◆ 1 cup ground meat
- ◆ 2 teaspoons oil
- ◆ 3 chopped potatoes
- ◆ 1 head of cabbage, chopped
- ◆ 1/4 cup cider vinegar

Heat oil and sauté onion and meat. Add potatoes and cook until softened. Add cabbage and cook until potatoes are very tender. Stir in vinegar. Serves 6.

Wheat Berry Melt

- ◆ 2 cups peeled and cubed butternut, squash
- ◆ I cup sliced carrots
- ◆ I cup sliced yellow squash
- ◆ 2 cups cooked wheat berries
- ◆ 2 tablespoons chopped scallion
- ◆ I tablespoon soy sauce
- ◆ 2 cups shredded monterey jack cheese

Steam butternut squash covered for 10 minutes. Add yelow squash and steam 5 minutes longer. Add wheat, scallions and soy sauce and transfer to a 2 qt. casserole dish. Sprinkle with cheese and bake at 375° until cheese is melted. Serves 4-6.

Kohlrabi Casserole

- ◆ 4 medium kohlrabi, peeled and julienned
- ◆ 2 chopped onions
- ◆ I lb. potatoes, scrubbed but not peeled
- ◆ 2 tablespoons oil
- ◆ I cup stock
- ◆ I tablespoon flour
- ◆ I/2 teaspoon salt
- ◆ 2 egg yolks
- ◆ I/2 cup milk
- ◆ 4 oz. grated gouda cheese
- ◆ 4 tablespoons fresh minced marjoram, or dried equivalent

Boil potatoes 30 minutes. Sauté onions in oil 3 minutes and add kohlrabi and sauté briefly. Pour I/2 cup stock over kohlrabi and braise covered 15 minutes. Whisk flour in remaining stock and add to kohlrabi. Continue cooking until thickened. Drain potatoes, cool, peel and slice. Add to kohlrabi along with salt. Separately, combine egg yolks, milk, cheese and vegetables. Garnish with marjoram. Serves 6-8.

Kasha and Kale

+ 2 tablespoons butter
+ I chopped onion
+ 2 minced garlic cloves
+ I/4 lb. sliced mushrooms
+ I/2 lb. fresh kale or collard greens, stemmed and cut thinly crosswise
+ I beaten egg
+ I cup kasha
+ 2 cups stock
+ I teaspoon lemon juice
+ I/4 teaspoon pepper

Sauté onion in butter 5 minutes. Add garlic and sauté I minute. Add mushrooms and sauté 8-10 minutes. During the last 2-3 minutes, add kale just until wilted. Remove to a bowl and raise heat to medium high. Add kasha to the beaten egg and cook in skillet, stirring constantly until egg and kasha separate, about 3 minutes. Add stock and boil. Simmer covered 10 minutes or until liquid is absorbed, then add reserved vegetables. Yields 6 cups.

Black Bean Burritos

+ 4 chopped carrots
+ I minced garlic clove
+ I teaspoon oil
+ I 3/4 cup (14 oz.) cooked black beans
+ I 1/4 cup chopped tomatoes
+ I/4 cup chopped green chiles
+ I teaspoon cumin
+ salt and pepper to taste

Sauté carrots and garlic in oil. Add the tomatoes and chiles and simmer 5 minutes. Add the beans and spices and simmer until thickened. Roll into a burrito or taco and serve with condiments.

Patties Gone Nuts

- ◆ 6 oz. chopped mushrooms
- ◆ 1 1/2 cup chopped carrots
- ◆ 1 1/2 cup minced onion
- ◆ 1 1/2 cup chopped seasonal squash
- ◆ 1/2 cup cashews
- ◆ 3 cups breadcrumbs
- ◆ 1/4 cup minced fresh parsley
- ◆ salt and pepper to taste

Sauté mushrooms 8-10 minutes and set aside. Combine the carrots, onion, squash and cashews in a processor and mix until it binds together. Transfer to bowl and add the mushrooms, breadcrumbs, parsley and seasonings until blended. Shape into 6 patties and pat flour on both sides. Chill until firm and then lightly fry in a skillet until browned.

Winter Harvest Dish

- ◆ 1 lb. parsnips
- ◆ 1 lb. carrots
- ◆ 3/4 lb. turnips
- ◆ 1 1/4 lb. rutabagas
- ◆ 1 sliced onion
- ◆ 6 whole peeled garlic cloves
- ◆ 3 tablespoons olive oil
- ◆ 1 tablespoon minced fresh dill
- ◆ 1 tablespoon fennel seeds
- ◆ 2 teaspoons salt
- ◆ 1 teaspoon pepper

Peel and trim ends of roots and chop in uniform pieces, 1/2-inch cubes. Combine roots, onion, garlic, oil, dill, fennel, salt and pepper. Using your hands, rub seasonings into vegetables until well coated. Transfer to an 18 x 12-inch roasting pan and cover with foil. Bake at 400° for 20 minutes. Remove foil and continue baking 30-40 minutes. Serves 8.

Potato Soup

French Style
- ♦ 2 tablespoons butter
- ♦ 2 large leeks, white and pale green parts only, thinly sliced
- ♦ 2 medium to large potatoes, peeled and chopped
- ♦ 4 cups stock
- ♦ 2 cups shredded carrots
- ♦ 1 teaspoon tarragon
- ♦ 1 1/2 cup half and half or milk
- ♦ salt and pepper to taste
- ♦ 3 tablespoons fresh chives

Melt butter in saucepan and sauté leeks 7 minutes. Add the potatoes and stock and boil. Simmer covered 15 minutes. Add carrots and tarragon and simmer 6-12 minutes until potatoes are tender. Purée in batches if necessary, in a processor or blender. If serving hot, heat the soup and add the milk. If serving cold, stir in the cold milk and season. Top with chives. Serves 4.

Sweet Potato Stew

- ♦ 3 tablespoons oil
- ♦ 1 cup minced onion
- ♦ 1 tablespoon chili powder
- ♦ 1 1/2 cup peeled and diced sweet potato
- ♦ 3-4 large tomatoes
- ♦ 2 cups cooked black beans
- ♦ 3 tablespoons fresh chopped cilantro
- ♦ salt and pepper to taste

Heat oil in a deep saucepan and sauté onion and garlic 4 minutes. Add chili powder, 1 cup water and the sweet potato. Simmer covered 10 minutes. Add tomatoes and beans, chunking up the tomatoes. Simmer uncovered 8 minutes. Mash one quarter of the beans against the side of the pan. Stir in seasonings. Serves 2-3.

Curried Winter Soup

- 1 chopped onion
- 3 minced garlic cloves
- 1 tablespoon olive oil
- 1-2 teaspoons curry
- 1 teaspoon cumin
- 1 teaspoon turmeric
- 8 cups stock
- 1/4 cup dry lentils
- 2 cups chopped tomatoes, including as much of the juice as possible
- 1 cup corn
- 1/4 cup brown rice or grain
- 1/2 cup elbow macaroni, optional
- 1 small halved spaghetti squash

Place squash halves, cut side down, on a lightly oiled baking sheet. Bake at 350° for 30 minutes, set aside, cool and chop. In a large pot sauté onions and garlic in oil. Add the seasonings and sauté 2 minutes. Add the stock and lentils and boil. Simmer and add tomatoes. After 10 minutes, add the rice and corn. After 25 minutes, add the macaroni and squash and simmer until rice and pasta are cooked. Serves 6.

Kale and Bean Soup

- 1/2 lb. dry navy beans
- water
- 2 tablespoons oil
- 3 diced celery stalks
- 2 medium sliced carrots
- 1 diced onion
- 1 minced garlic clove
- 6 cups stock
- 1/2 teaspoon pepper
- 2 1/4 cup cooked kale or spinach
- 1 cup cooked small shell pasta, optional
- Parmesan, optional

Add enough water to the beans and cover them by 2 inches. Boil 5 minutes, remove and let stand covered 1 hour, then drain. Heat oil and sauté celery, onion, carrot and garlic in a large pot for 5 minutes. Add beans, stock and pepper and boil. Simmer covered 1 hour. With a slotted spoon, remove 1 cup of the beans and mash them. Return to pot and add kale. Boil, then simmer 10 minutes. Add pasta and Parmesan. Yields 8 cups.

Squash Soup

South American Soup

- ◆ 4 oz. flank steak, cut in 1/2-inch cubes
- ◆ 1 tablespoon oil
- ◆ 1 small butternut squash
- ◆ 1 chopped onion
- ◆ 2 1/2 cups stock
- ◆ 1 1/2 cup pureed tomatoes

- ◆ 2 teaspoons soy sauce
- ◆ 1 teaspoon minced fresh marjoram
- ◆ 1 teaspoon minced fresh thyme
- ◆ 1/4 teaspoon hot pepper sauce

Heat oil in a 3 qt. saucepan and brown steak. Remove. Peel, seed and cube the squash. Add to the saucepan along with onion and simmer covered for 15 minutes. Add the steak, stock, tomatoes, soy sauce, herbs and hot sauce. Simmer covered 15 minutes. Serves 4.

Sweet Bean Soup

Serve hot or cold.

- ◆ 1 teaspoon olive oil
- ◆ 1 cup chopped onion
- ◆ 2 minced garlic cloves
- ◆ 3-4 julienned carrots
- ◆ 1 tablespoon fresh rosemary
- ◆ 4 cups stock

- ◆ 1 medium firm pear, peeled, cored and chopped
- ◆ 2 cups cooked white or preferred bean
- ◆ salt and pepper to taste
- ◆ 1/4 cup chopped fresh parsley
- ◆ 1 cup milk, if serving cold

Heat oil in medium stock pot and sauté onion 4 minutes. Add the garlic and sauté 1 minute. Add the stock, carrots and rosemary and bring to a boil. Simmer covered 10 minutes. Add the pear and beans and cook 15 minutes longer. Purée soup, by batches if necessary, in a processor or blender and season with salt and pepper. Return to pot to heat if serving hot, bring to refrigerator if serving cold. Serves 4.

Creamy Sweet Potato-Leek Soup

- 2 peeled and cubed sweet potatoes
- 2 leeks, topped, tailed and chopped
- I chopped onion
- I chopped shallot
- 2 cups vegetable stock
- 1/4 teaspoon nutmeg
- I cup milk
- salt to taste

Bring all ingredients, except milk, to a boil and simmer covered 25 minutes. Purée in a blender or processor, adding milk as you go. Serves 4.

Wild Rice and Parsnip Soup

- I tablespoon oil
- I chopped onion
- I chopped leek
- I lb. finely chopped parsnips
- I bay leaf
- 3 minced garlic cloves
- 4 cups vegetable stock
- 1/4 cup uncooked wild rice
- 3 tablespoons fresh thyme
- salt to taste

Warm oil over medium heat in a large soup pot. Add onion, leek, parsnips, bay leaf and garlic. Sauté 8 minutes. Add stock, rice, thyme and boil. Simmer covered I hour. Serves 4.

La's Split Pea Soup

- I lb. split peas
- 3 qt. water
- carrots, celery and potatoes, to preference
- 1-2 bay leaves
- 1/2 cup onion
- I cubed ham steak

Can double and/or freeze. Combine all ingredients and simmer 2 hours. Salt to taste.

Alpine Village House Soup

- 2 qt. stock
- 2 teaspoons celery salt
- 2 teaspoons multi herb seasoning
- 1 lb. ground cooked chicken
- 1 minced onion
- 2 teaspoons salt
- 2 minced carrots
- 1/2 cup oil
- 1 cup flour

Can be doubled and/or frozen. Combine all but the oil and flour and boil for 30 minutes. To prepare roux, heat oil until smoking and add the flour with a wire whisk. The oil and flour should be the consistency of mashed potatoes. Add the roux to the soup. The soup should be smooth, so you may need to purée in batches in a processor or blender. Serve hot.

Winter Sides and Breads

Cranberry Bread

- 2 cups wheat flour
- 1 1/2 teaspoon baking soda
- 1/2 teaspoon salt
- 1/2 cup orange juice
- 1 tablespoon grated orange rind
- 2 tablespoons oil
- hot water
- 1/2 cup honey
- 1 beaten egg
- 1 cup coarsely chopped cranberries
- 1/2 cup chopped walnuts or pecans

Mix the flour, soda, powder and salt together. Separately combine the juice, rind, oil and enough hot water to make 3/4 cup liquid. Add to dry ingredients. Add honey and egg and fold in cranberries and nuts. Pour into a greased loaf pan and bake at 325° for 1 hour.

Orange Nut Bread

- ◆ 1 1/2-3 teaspoons yeast
- ◆ 1 cup warm orange juice
- ◆ 1 tablespoon honey
- ◆ 1 tablespoon butter
- ◆ 3/4 teaspoon salt
- ◆ 2 eggs
- ◆ 3 cups wheat flour
- ◆ 1/2 tablespoons grated orange rind
- ◆ 1/2 cup raisins, optional
- ◆ 1/4 cup chopped walnuts

Dissolve yeast in juice with honey in a large bowl until bubbly. Add butter, salt, eggs and half the flour and beat for several minutes. Add remaining flour to make a soft dough. Knead in the rind, raisins and walnuts for 5-10 minutes. Let rise until doubled. Place in a greased loaf pan and bake at 375° for 45 minutes.

Apple Gingerbread

- ◆ 1/2 cup softened butter
- ◆ 2 eggs
- ◆ 2/3 cups molasses or honey
- ◆ 2 cups wheat flour
- ◆ 1 1/2 teaspoon ground ginger
- ◆ 1/2 teaspoon each cinnamon and nutmeg
- ◆ 1/4 teaspoon ground cloves
- ◆ 3/4 cup milk
- ◆ 1 1/4 cup grated apple
- ◆ whipped cream, optional

Cream butter, eggs and molasses. Separately, combine dry ingredients and add to creamed mixture, alternately with milk. Stir in grated apple. Pour into a 9 x 9-inch cake pan. Bake at 350° for 45 minutes. Top with whipped cream.

Teff Spoon Bread

- ♦ 2 cups cooked teff
- ♦ I cup milk
- ♦ 2 tablespoons honey
- ♦ 2 tablespoons melted butter
- ♦ 3 eggs, separated
- ♦ 2 teaspoons baking powder
- ♦ I teaspoon salt

Combine teff, milk, honey, butter, egg yolks, baking powder and salt. Separately, beat egg whites until stiff. Fold in teff mixture. Turn into greased I 1/2 qt. dish. Bake 50 minutes at 350° until puffed and browned.

Millet Biscuits with Rosemary

- ♦ I cup wheat flour
- ♦ I 1/2 cup unbleached flour
- ♦ I teaspoon baking soda
- ♦ 1/2 teaspoon salt
- ♦ I teaspoon cream of tartar
- ♦ I-2 teaspoons ground rosemary
- ♦ I cup cooked millet
- ♦ 2 tablespoons oil
- ♦ 2 egg whites
- ♦ 1/2 cup plain yogurt

Combine flours, baking soda, salt, cream of tartar, rosemary and millet in a large bowl. In a medium bowl whisk the oil, egg whites and yogurt. Combine ingredients together and knead the dough until smooth. Roll out and cut or drop on a greased cookie sheet. Bake at 425° for 15 minutes.

Parsnips with Garlic and Breadcrumbs

- 1 lb. sliced parsnips
- 1 teaspoon olive oil
- 2 minced garlic cloves
- 2 slices wheat bread, rubbed into crumbs
- 4 tablespoons minced fresh basil
- salt to taste

Steam parsnips 10-12 minutes. Drain and pat dry. Heat oil in a skillet on medium high and sauté garlic, crumbs, basil and salt 2 minutes. Stir in parsnips. For a main dish, serve over pasta. Serves 4.

Garlic Mashed Parsnips

- 1 lb. parsnips, peeled and chopped
- 6 sliced garlic cloves
- 1 teaspoon oil
- 1/2 cup plain yogurt
- 3 tablespoons minced fresh parsley
- salt to taste

Steam parsnips and garlic in boiling water 12-14 minutes. Drain and pat dry. Mash both in a medium bowl, adding oil, yogurt, salt and parsley as you go. Serves 6.

Leek Braised Parsnips

- 2 cups vegetable stock
- 1 bay leaf
- 2 leeks, topped, tailed and sliced
- 1 lb. sliced parsnips
- juice of 1 lemon
- 2 teaspoons oil
- 3 tsp. minced fresh tarragon
- salt to taste

Heat stock on high in a large skillet. At simmer, add the bay leaf, leeks, garlic and parsnips. Simmer covered until parsnips are tender, about 9 minutes. Remove leeks and parsnips and arrange in a serving bowl. In a small bowl combine the lemon juice, oil, tarragon and salt. Sprinkle over parsnips. May serve on a bed of kale or collards. Serves 4.

Warmed Beets

♦ I tablespoon butter I tablespoon flour
♦ 1/2 cup vegetable stock
♦ 1/2 cup milk
♦ I tablespoon Dijon style mustard
♦ I teaspoon minced chives
♦ 3 teaspoons minced fresh tarragon
♦ 8 beets, sliced and cooked

Heat stock, milk and butter in saucepan. Whisk in flour and simmer, stirring constantly for 1-2 minutes until thickened. Add spices and drizzle over beets. Serves 8.

Mashed Sweet Potatoes with Orange and Nutmeg

♦ 3 peeled and cubed sweet potatoes
♦ 2 sliced carrots
♦ 1/4 cup orange juice
♦ 1/4 teaspoon grated orange rind
♦ 1/4 teaspoon nutmeg
♦ salt to taste

Steam the potatoes and carrots 20 minutes. In a medium bowl, combine them with the remaining ingredients and mash. Serves 6.

Buckwheat Pudding

Very simple
♦ 2 cups cooked buckwheat
♦ I cup milk
♦ 1/4 cup dark honey
♦ I teaspoon vanilla
♦ 1/4 teaspoon lemon zest
♦ salt to taste

Oil a I qt. baking dish and combine all ingredients in the dish. Bake at 350° for 45 minutes until set. Serves 4.

Millet Stuffed Apples

- 1/2 cup millet
- 1 cup boiling water
- 4 large apples
- 1 1/2 cup cottage cheese
- 3 teaspoons raisins
- 2 teaspoons shredded

- muenster cheese
- 1/4 teaspoon cinnamon
- 1/8 teaspoon nutmeg
- 1/2 cup water
- 1/4 cup apple juice

Heat saucepan and toast millet until brown. Add water and simmer covered 20 minutes. Cut 1/2 inch from the top of each apple and remove core. Hollow out apples with a spoon. Chop one cup of apple flesh and reserve tops and remaining flesh; set aside. In a blender or processor, blend cottage cheese. Combine cottage cheese in a bowl with chopped apples, raisins, muenster, cinnamon, nutmeg and cooked millet. Grease a 9 x 9-inch baking dish. Spoon millet mixture into apples. Spread remaining mixture into the bottom of the dish and top with apples. Add the 1/2 cup water and apple juice and bake at 350° for 35 minutes. Serves 4.

Mashed Potatoes and Amaranth

- 1 lb. (3 medium sized) potatoes, peeled and cut into quarters
- 1/4 cup butter
- 1/4 cup minced onion
- 3/4 cup half and half
- 2 tablespoons sour cream
- 3/4 cup cooked amaranth
- salt and pepper to taste

Boil potatoes in water for 30 minutes, then drain. Meanwhile, heat 1 tablespoon butter in a small skillet and sauté onion 4 minutes; set aside. Mash potatoes in the saucepan with 3 tablespoons butter, half and half, sour cream, salt and pepper. Stir in amaranth and onion. Stir rapidly over low heat until combined. Serves 6.

Stuffed Potatoes

- ◆ 5 baked potatoes, hot from the oven
- ◆ I cup plain yogurt
- ◆ I cup shredded cheddar cheese
- ◆ 3 teaspoons butter
- ◆ 2 tablespoons milk
- ◆ 2 teaspoons minced onion
- ◆ 1/2 teaspoon salt
- ◆ dash of pepper
- ◆ 1/2 cup crumbed bacon, optional

Slice potatoes lengthwise in half. Scoop out centers, reserving shells. Beat potatoes in a mixer with remaining ingredients. Stuff into reserved shells and place on a baking sheet and bake at 400° for 15 minutes.

Stuffed Yams

- ◆ 6 medium yams
- ◆ 1/4 teaspoon nutmeg
- ◆ 1/4 teaspoon ground cloves
- ◆ I tablespoon vanilla
- ◆ I tablespoon almond extract
- ◆ 2 teaspoons honey
- ◆ I cup plain yogurt
- ◆ I tablespoon butter
- ◆ I beaten egg

Scrub yams and make a 2-inch slit in the center of each one and place in a baking dish. Bake at 400° for 1 1/4 hours. Cut in half lengthwise, scooping out centers into a large bowl, reserving skins. Mash yam flesh with remaining ingredients and fill yam shells. Bake at 350° for 15 minutes.

Beet Greens with Potatoes and Rosemary

- 2 teaspoons olive oil
- 2 minced garlic cloves
- 3 teaspoons minced fresh rosemary
- 2 medium cubed and steamed potatoes
- 2 cups chopped beet greens
- salt to taste

Heat oil and sauté all ingredients until greens are wilted, about 4 minutes. Serve over rice or grains. Serves 4.

Winter Desserts

Polynesian Bars

- 2 cups chopped dates
- I tablespoon vanilla
- 2 1/2 cups grated apples with juice
- I cup wheat flour
- I cup shredded coconut
- 1/2 cup chopped walnuts or preferred nut
- 3 cups rolled oats
- I cup orange juice
- 1/4 cup honey
- 1/4 cup oil

Cook dates, vanilla and undrained apple in saucepan until thickened. Separately, combine the flour, coconut, walnuts, oats, juice, honey and oil – this is your base. Press half the base mixture into a greased 9 x 12-inch baking pan. Spread with date mixture, top with remaining base mixture. Bake at 350° for 30-40 minutes. Cool and cut bars.

Date Bars

- 1 lb. chopped dates
- 1 1/2 cup shredded coconut
- 1/2 cup butter
- 1/2 cup water
- 1/4 cup honey
- 2 1/2 cups rolled oats
- 2/3 cups chopped nuts
- 1 teaspoon vanilla

Cook dates, coconut, butter, water and honey until thickened. Add remaining ingredients. Spread in buttered 9 x 9-inch pan and chill 2 hours.

Snow Cream

- 2 beaten eggs, optional
- 2 cups room temperature milk
- 3/4 cup honey
- 1/4 teaspoon salt
- 1 tablespoon vanilla
- fresh fruit juices to taste
- bucket of fresh, clean snow

Beat eggs and milk, then blend in honey. Add salt, vanilla and juices. Combine with enough snow to fill a gallon container. Serve immediately as the snow melts quickly.

Date Nut Cake

- 1 cup chopped dates
- 1/2 cup chopped walnuts
- 3/4 cup honey
- 1 1/4 cup wheat flour
- 1 teaspoon baking soda
- salt to taste
- 1 cup boiling water
- 1 tablespoon butter
- 1 teaspoon vanilla

Combine dates, walnuts, flour, soda and salt. Separately, combine water, butter and vanilla in a small bowl. Add to date mixture and combine well. Spoon into a greased and floured 9 x 9-inch pan. Bake at 350° for 30-40 minutes. Garnish with whipped cream if desired.

Apple Crisp

+ 6 green or golden apples, cored and sliced with skins
+ I tablespoon melted butter
+ 1/3 teaspoon cinnamon
+ 2 tablespoons butter
+ 1/2 cup wheat flour
+ I 1/2 cup granola

Place sliced apples in an 8-inch square glass pan, pour melted butter over them and sprinkle cinnamon on top. In a separate bowl, cut the solid butter into flour and mix until crumbly. Fold in granola and mix well. Sprinkle over apples and bake at 350° for 40 minutes. Cool and serve.

Apple Brown Betty

+ 2 1/2 lbs. (6-8) seasonal apples, peeled and cut into 1/2-inch thick slices
+ 3/4 cup honey or maple syrup
+ 2 1/2 tablespoons lemon juice
+ I teaspoon grated lemon rind
+ 1/2 cup raisins, optional
+ 1/4 teaspoon cinnamon
+ 1/2 cup apple juice (use 3/4 cup if apples are dry)
+ 3 cups breadcrumbs
+ 1/4 cup oil
+ 3/4 cup honey or maple syrup
+ 1/2 cup wheat germ
+ 1/2 teaspoon cinnamon

Put apples in a large bowl. Combine honey, lemon juice and rind. Add to the apples and toss. Add raisins, cinnamon and apple juice. Turn into a shallow baking dish. Toast breadcrumbs in oil. Remove from heat and add 1/3 cup honey, then add the wheat germ and cinnamon. Cover apples with topping. Bake at 325° for 45 minutes on middle rack.

Apple Pudding

- ◆ 1/4 cup apple juice or water
- ◆ 2 cups chopped seasonal apples
- ◆ 1 cup raisins
- ◆ 1 cup honey or maple syrup
- ◆ 1 egg
- ◆ 1 teaspoon cinnamon
- ◆ 1 teaspoon baking soda
- ◆ 1 cup chopped nuts, optional
- ◆ 1 1/2 cup wheat flour
- ◆ 1 teaspoon salt
- ◆ 1/2 cup oil

Beat egg, oil, juice and honey and pour over combined apples, raisins and nuts. Stir in cinnamon, soda, salt and flour. Put in an 8-inch square dish and bake at 350° for 30 minutes.

Apple Pie

No Bake
- ◆ 1-2 finely chopped apples
- ◆ 1/4 teaspoon cinnamon
- ◆ 1/8 teaspoon nutmeg
- ◆ 1/2 teaspoon lemon juice

Combine ingredients. Pour into pie shell (recipe below) and chill.

Pecan Walnut Pie Shell

- ◆ 1/4 cup pecans
- ◆ 1/4 cup walnuts
- ◆ 4 dates

Combine in a processor or blender and press into a pie plate.

Ginger Carrot Cake

- 3/4 cup apple juice
- 1/2 cup oil
- 1 1/2 cup raisins
- 1/2 cup maple syup
- 1 1/2 cup grated carrots
- 2 teaspoons grated ginger
- 2 cups wheat flour
- 1 teaspoon baking powder
- 1 teaspoon baking soda
- 1 teaspoon cinnamon
- 1/2 teaspoon nutmeg
- 1/2 teaspoon salt
- 1 cup chopped walnuts

Combine the juice, oil, 1/2 cup raisins and maple syrup in a blender and pulse until smooth. Add carrots and ginger and pulse to mix. Whisk the flour, baking powder and soda, cinnamon, nutmeg and salt together in a large bowl. Add the apple juice mixture and combine using as few strokes as possible. Fold in remaining raisins and walnuts. Pour into a greased and floured 8-inch square dish. Bake at 350° for 35-45 minutes.

Caramelized Pears

- 3/4 cup butter
- 4 large pears, peeled, cored and cut in quarters
- 2 tablespoons orange juice
- 2 tablespoons honey
- 1 tablespoon crystallized ginger

Melt the butter in a skillet and add the pears. Add the orange juice and heat, turning pears until softened. Add the honey and ginger and increase the heat, stirring until it forms a caramel sauce. Serve warm with the sauce poured over it.

Pear Upside Down Cake

- 1 cup flour
- 1 teaspoon baking powder
- 1/4 teaspoon baking soda
- 1/4 teaspoon salt
- 1/2 cup honey
- 1 egg
- 2 tablespoons melted butter
- 2 tablespoons orange juice

topping (recipe follows)

Combine flour, baking powder and soda and salt. In a small bowl, combine the honey, egg, butter and orange juice. Add to the flour and spread mixture over topping. Bake at 375° for 30 minutes. Cool, flip over, cut and serve.

Pear Topping

- 1 peeled and thinly sliced pear
- 1 tablespoon flour
- 2 teaspoons grated orange peel
- 1 teaspoon cinnamon
- 1/2 cup honey

Arrange pears in a fan shape in the bottom of a greased pie plate. Sprinkle with flour, orange peel and cinnamon. Drizzle evenly with honey.

Recipe Favorites

INDEX

YEAR ROUND

YEAR ROUND GRAINS, RICE, AND BEANS

ADZUKI BEANS 8
AMARANTH 1
ANASAZI BEANS 9
ARBORIO RICE 6
BARLEY, PEARLED 1
BARLEY, WHOLE 1
BASMATI BROWN RICE 6
BASMATI WHITE RICE 6
BLACK BEANS 9
BLACK EYED PEAS 9
BROWN LONG AND MEDIUM
    GRAIN RICE 7
BROWN SHORT GRAIN RICE 7
BUCKWHEAT, WHOLE 1
BULGAR WHEAT 2
CANELLI BEANS 10
CRANBERRY BEANS 9
FAVA BEANS 10
GARBANZO BEANS 10
GREAT NORTHERN BEANS 10
JASMINE BROWN RICE 7
JASMINE WHITE RICE 7
KAMUT 2
KIDNEY BEANS 11
LENTILS 11
LIMA BEAN 11
MILLET 2
MUNG BEAN 11
NAVY BEANS 11
NO COOKING/RAW METHOD
    FOR GRAINS, RICE AND BEANS 6
OAT GROATS 2
OATS, QUICK 3
OATS, ROLLED 3
OATS, STEEL CUT 3
PEAS, SPLIT 12
PEAS, WHOLE 12
PINTO BEANS 12
QUINOA 4
RED BEANS 12
RYE BERRIES 4

SOY BEANS - BEIGE OR
    BLACK 12
SPELT 4
SUSHI RICE 7
SWEET RICE 8
TEFF BERRIES 5
WEHANI RICE 8
WHEAT - CROCKPOT METHOD 6
WHEAT - THERMOS METHOD 5
WHEAT BERRIES 5
WHEAT, CRACKED 5
WILD RICE 8

YEAR ROUND BASICS

APPLE BUTTER 25
APPLESAUCE 26
BEAN PUREE 25
BUCKWHEAT CREPES 21
BUTTER 15
BUTTER SUBSTITUTE 16
CASHEW MILK 19
CATSUP 16
CHINESE BARBEQUE SAUCE 17
DATE SUGAR 20
DIASTATIC MALT 20
EASY OIL CRUST 21
GRAHAM CRACKER PIE CRUST 24
GRAHAM CRACKERS 24
HUMMUS 17
MAYONNAISE 16
MULTI GRAIN PASTA 14
NATURAL DYES 26
NO CREAM SOUP BASE 22
NO CREAM SOUP BASE II 22
NUT BUTTERS 18
PEANUT BUTTER 18
PESTO SAUCE 25
PITA POCKETS 14
REFRIED BEANS 17
RICE OR GRAIN CRUST 21
SESAME MILK 19
SODA CRACKERS 23
SOYMILK 19
WHEAT CREPES 20

INDEX

WHEAT NUTS 24
WHEAT PASTA 13
WHEAT PASTA - EGOLESS 13
WHEAT THINS 23
WHEAT TORTILLAS 15
WONTON SKINS OR EGG ROLL
    WRAPPERS 22

YEAR ROUND BREAKFASTS
BLENDER PANCAKES OR
    WAFFLES 28
FRUIT SYRUPS 30
GRAIN MUFFINS 29
GRANOLA 27
MILLET BREAKFAST CEREAL 29
MIXED GRAIN CEREAL 29
MUESLI 30
PEANUT BUTTER GRANOLA 28
YEAR ROUND BREAKFASTSTAPLES 27

YEAR ROUND LUNCHES
GARBANZO AND PEANUT SOUP 32
LENTIL SALAD 31
ORANGE SALAD DRESSING 33
POTATO-LESS SALAD 32
UN MEATBALLS 31
VINAIGRETTE DRESSING 33
WHEAT LOAF 32

YEAR ROUND DINNERS
BAKED BEAN CASSEROLE 34
BARLEY AND ALMOND CASSEROLE 35
COUSCOUS OR QUINOA AND
    LENTILS 37
FRIED RICE 36
KASHA VARNISKAS 35
QUINOA EGGDROP SOUP 36
WHEAT BURGER 37

YEAR ROUND SIDES AND BREADS
BAGELS 38

BOSTON BAKED BEANS 43
CHALLAH BREAD 38
CHILI NUTS 43
CRESCENT ROLLS 42
ENGLISH MUFFINS 41
HAMBURGER BUNS 40
HARVEST BREAD 39
LIMA BEAN SIDE DISH 42
SPROUTED WHEAT BREAD 39
TOASTED MILLET 43

YEAR ROUND DESSERTS
BETTER THAN RICE KRISPIE
    TREATS 51
BROWNIES 50
CREOLE DOUGHNUTS 46
CULVA 51
DEVIL'S FOOD CAKE 49
FRUIT LEATHER 48
GLAZE FOR COOKIES,
    DOUGHNUTS AND CAKES 46
HONEY GLAZE 50
ICE CREAM CONES 45
MILK FREE DOUGHNUTS 46
NUT BUTTER BARS 49
OAT CAKE 47
ROB ROY COOKIES 44
VANILLA YOGURT TOPPING 50
WHEAT CAKE 44

SPRING
SPRING BREAKFASTS
APRICOT QUINOA-MILLET CEREAL 55
CHEESE BREAD 53
EASY STRAWBERRY JAM 55
FRUIT CHEESE TOAST 54
NUTTY FRUITY FRENCH TOAST 53
RHUBARB MUFFINS 54

SPRING LUNCHES
ARTICHOKE AND ASPARAGUS
    SALAD 57
ARTICHOKE GONDOLAS 56

INDEX

BRITISH POTATO SALAD 56
BULGAR DISH 57
CORN FRITTERS 60
CORNSICLES 60
CREAMY BEET SALAD 59
CURRIED FRY BITES 58
INDIAN PUDDING 62
KASHISALAD.. 58
LINGUINE AND SPINACH 55
PEAS AND CHEESE 59
POLENTA 61
SPINACH PIE... 59

SPRING DINNERS
ARTICHOKE QUICHE 63
BARLEY, BEAN, AND CORN
    BURRITOS 70
BLACK BEAN AND SPINACH
    SOUP.. 67
EGGS A LA GOLDEN ROD 67
MILLET SALAD 66
NASIGORENG 65
OVERNIGHT ONION SOUP.................... 69
PENNE WITH GARLIC ASPARAGUS 63
POLENTA AND BLACK BEAN
    CASSEROLE.................................... 71
POLENTA TORTE 68
SALMON WITH CHILE AND LIME 64
SALMON WITH HERB PASTE 64
SPAGHETTI SQUASH.............................. 69
SPINACH MUSHROOM CREPES 66
SWISS CHARD PIE 68
UN CHICKEN FRIED DINNER
    CASSEROLE.................................... 71
SPRING SIDES AND BREADS
COTTAGE CHEESE 76
CREAM CHEESE OR RICOTTA
    CHEESE 75
EGG FOO YUNG 76
GREEN BEANS WITH DILL AND
    ALMONDS 73
ITALIAN FRIED RICE.............................. 73
POPOVERS a.k.a. YORKSHIRE PUDDING ... 72

RHUBARB BREAD 72
SPINACH RISOTTO 73
SPROUT BALL.. 74
SPROUT DIP 75
STUFFED PEACHES 74

SPRING DESSERTS
BROWN RICE PUDDING 81
CAROB ALMOND CAKE 81
CHEESECAKE 78
CREAM CHEESE FROSTING 79
FUDGE PIE 79
HALF MOONS 79
PEACH SOUFFLE 77
PEANUT BUTTER SATIN 78
SPONGE CAKE 80
STRAWBERRY PIE 77
STRAWBERRY RHUBARB
    DESSERT SAUCE 78

SUMMER
SUMMER BREAKFASTS
BANANA PANCAKES 86
BREAKFAST BARS 84
BUCKWHEAT MUSH 84
CHERRY MAPLE CRUNCH 83
FRESH FRUIT TEA 85
LEMONADE WITH A TWIST 85
PINEAPPLE MUFFINS.............................. 83
TROPICAL MUSH 84

SUMMER LUNCHES
BANANA PEANUT BUTTER
    "SANDWICHES" 94
BEAN PESTO 89
COLESLAW 92
CORN AND PEA SOUP 93
CORN SALAD WITH TOMATO
    DRESSING 87
CURRIED MILLET SALAD 89
FRIED GREEN TOMATOES 94

INDEX

KUMQUAT AND SNOW PEA
   RICE SALAD 91
MOROCCAN SALAD 90
NO CREAM OF MUSHROOM SOUP 93
PEACH AND WALNUT SALAD 88
RICE, BEAN, AND CORN SALAD 86
ZUCCHINI CORN SOUP 88
ZUCCHINI MILK 88
ZUCCHINI "PASTA" 87

SUMMER DINNERS

ARROZ CON FRIJOLES 102
BLACK BEAN BURGERS 95
BULGAR AND BEANS 95
QUINOA STEW 97
RAGOUT 99
RED BEANS AND RICE 103
RICE 'N' PEAS 99
SQUASHED NUTS CASSEROLE 104
STUFFED ZUCCHINI 97
TABBOULEH 100
TACO SALAD 102
TACOS 96
TAMALE PIE 104
VEGETABLE TERRINE 101
WHITE CORN TORTILLA SOUP 105
WILD RICE AND BEAN SALAD 96
WILD RICE AND PINE NUTS 98
ZUCCHINI STUFFED MUSHROOMS ... 103

SUMMER SIDES AND BREADS

APPLE DATE BREAD 106
BANANA NUT BREAD 106
CORN AND BLACK BEAN SALAD 112
CORN CHIPS 110
CORN RELISH 110
CORN TORTILLAS 108
CORN TORTILLAS II 108
INDIAN RICE 111
MASA 108
STUFFED ONIONS 109
SUMMER SQUASH ROLLS 107
SWEET AND SOUR SAUCE 112

SWEET CORNBREAD 107
TROPICAL COMPOTE 109
WILD RICE AND ENDIVE SALAD 111
WILD RICE WITH APRICOTS
   AND PECANS 112

SUMMER DESSERTS

BANANA BARLEY COOKIES 117
BANANA CAKE 116
BANANA CREAM SHAKE 116
BANANA ICE MILK 113
CINNAMON PEACH COBBLER 115
FROZEN PINEAPPLE YOGURT 113
FRUITY GRAIN SALAD 115
LEMON BERRY ICE CREAM 114
MAPLE POPCORN 119
PASSION FRUIT FREEZE 114
PEACH PIE 118
PEANUT BUTTER CLUSTERS 118
RHUBARB PIE 116
STRAWBERRY PIE 117
STRAWBERRY SHERBET 114

FALL
FALL BREAKFASTS

APPLE AND OAT BARS 122
DATE NUT MUFFINS 121
ORANGE MUFFINS 121
POTATO AND PEPPER SAUTE 123
SWEET PUMPKIN CORNBREAD 122

FALL LUNCHES

BARLEY "RISOTTO" 124
BROCCOLI WALNUT
      SANDWICH ROLL 128
CALIFORNIA SALAD 125
FRUITY QUINOA SALAD 126
JICAMA SALAD 127
QUINOA MELODY 129
RED BEANS AND BARLEY 123
RICE, CORN AND LENTIL SALAD 124
SIX LAYER CASSEROLE 128
TUNA AND BEAN SALAD 127

INDEX

TUSCAN BREAD SALAD 129
WALDORF SALAD 126
WHEAT BERRY TOMATO SALAD 125

FALL DINNERS
BARLEY AND BEANS 131
BEAN BURGERS 130
BEANBURRITOS 131
BROCCOLI, POTATO AND
    LEEK SOUP 140
CHEESE ENCHILADAS 137
CHILE QUINOA CASSEROLE 136
CORN AND CABBAGE SKILLET 137
CREAM OF BROCCOLI SOUP 139
FALL CASSEROLE................................. 132
FEIJOADA.. 134
GERMAN RICE SALAD 136
GRAIN STUFFING 132
GRAIN VEGETABLE SOUP 141
MASHED POTATO AND ROASTED
    VEGETABLE ENCHILADAS 139
MEATLESS SLOPPY JOES 133
PUMPKIN BISQUE 141
RICE AND BLACK EYED PEA
    SALAD 138
SPLIT PEA SOUP 140
STUFFED ACORN SQUASH 130
SWEET SQUASH BISQUE 142
VEGETABLE PIE 135

FALL SIDES AND BREADS
BAKED ONIONS WITH
    PUMPKIN 146
CARROT BREAD 143
CRANBERRY, ORANGE, AND
    RASPBERRY JAM 150
CRANBERRY PEARS 145
CRANBERRY SAUCE 149
GREEN BEAN CREOLE 149
GREEN CHILE SAUCE 148
HOT PEPPER SALSA 146
INDIAN GREEN BEANS 149
POOR MAN'S CAVIAR......................... 147

PUMPKIN CORNBREAD 145
QUINCE CUPS.................................... 148
RICE CAKES....................................... 147
RYE BREAD 144
SWEET AND SOUR SAUCE 150

FALL DESSERTS
APPLE SPICE CAKE 155
AVOCADO DESSERT 154
CARROT CAKE 153
CREAMED PERSIMMON 151
PEAR SAUCE 151
PERSIMMON PUDDING 151
PUMPKIN BARS 152
PUMPKIN MOUSSE 155
PUMPKIN WALNUT PIE 152
PUMPKIN-LESS PIE 154
RASPBERRY SLUSH 155
VANILLA POACHED PEARS 150

WINTER
WINTER BREAKFASTS
APPLE BREAD 158
APPLE MUFFINS 157
APPLE PECAN STICKY BUNS 159
CARROT SPICE MUFFINS 157

WINTER LUNCHES
BASIL POTATO SALAD......................... 165
BEANS AND GREENS 165
BEET AND CARROT SLAW 166
BUCKWHEAT PILAF WITH
    GARLIC AND LEEK 160
CREAM OF SPLIT PEA SOUP 164
CURRIED BROWN RICE...................... 166
FAJITAS 160
LIMA BEAN CHOWDER....................... 164
O'BRIEN POTATOES 161
POTATO AND ONION FRITTATA 163
POTATO AND TEFF LATKES 165
WHEAT BERRY SCAMPI 161
WHOLE MEAL SALAD 163
WINTER SALAD 162

INDEX

WINTER DINNERS

ALPINE VILLAGE HOUSE SOUP 179
BARLEY AND VEGGIE BAKE 170
BLACK BEAN BURRITOS 173
BUBBLE AND SQUEAK 171
CABBAGE ROLLS 169
CHICK PEA AND POTATO CURRY 167
CREAMY SWEET
      POTATO-LEEK SOUP 178
CURRIED WINTER SOUP 176
ITALIAN RICE 168
KALE AND BEAN SOUP 176
KASHA AND KALE 173
KOHLRABI CASSEROLE 172
LA'S SPLIT PEA SOUP 178
NOT QUITE SPAGHETTI AND
      MEAT SAUCE 170
PATTIES GONE NUTS 174
POTATO PIE 171
POTATO SOUP 175
SQUASH SOUP 177
SWEET BEAN SOUP 177
SWEET POTATO STEW 175
SWEET POTATOES WITH
      APPLES AND CINNAMON 167
WHEAT BERRY MELT 172
WILD RICE AND PARSNIP SOUP 178
WINTER HARVEST DISH 174

WINTER SIDES AND BREADS

APPLE GINGERBREAD 180
BEET GREENS WITH
      POTATOES AND ROSEMARY 186
BUCKWHEAT PUDDING 183
CRANBERRY BREAD 179
GARLIC MASHED PARSNIPS 182
LEEK BRAISED PARSNIPS 182
MASHED POTATOES AND
      AMARANTH 184
MASHED SWEET POTATOES WITH
      ORANGE AND NUTMEG 183
MILLET BISCUITS WITH
      ROSEMARY 181

MILLET STUFFED APPLES 184
ORANGE NUT BREAD 180
PARSNIPS WITH GARLIC AND
      BREADCRUMBS 182
STUFFED POTATOES 185
STUFFED YAMS 185
TEFF SPOON BREAD 181
WARMED BEETS 183

WINTER DESSERTS

APPLE BROWN BETTY 188
APPLE CRISP 188
APPLE PIE 189
APPLE PUDDING 189
CARAMELIZED PEARS 190
DATE BARS 187
DATE NUT CAKE 187
GINGER CARROT CAKE 190
PEAR UPSIDE DOWN CAKE 191
POLYNESIAN BARS 186
SNOW CREAM 187

23843940R00127

Made in the USA
Lexington, KY
25 June 2013